JUANITA CARBERRY
WITH NICOLA TYRER

———————◆———————

CHILD OF
HAPPY VALLEY

A Memoir

Complete and Unabridged

KT-562-222

CHARNWOOD
Leicester

First published in Great Britain in 1999 by
William Heinemann Limited
London

First Charnwood Edition
published 2001
by arrangement with
Heinemann
The Random House Group Limited
London

British Library CIP Data

Carberry, Juanita, 1925—
Child of Happy Valley: a memoir.—
Large print ed.—
Charnwood library series
1. Carberry, Juanita, 1925— 2.Women—Kenya
3. British—Kenya 4. Large type books 5. Kenya
I. Title II. Tyrer, Nicola
967.6′203′092

ISBN 0–7089–9255–2

C15147102

Published by
F. A. Thorpe (Publishing)
Anstey, Leicestershire

Set by Words & Graphics Ltd.
Anstey, Leicestershire
Printed and bound in Great Britain by
T. J. International Ltd., Padstow, Cornwall

This book is printed on acid-free paper

Juanita Carberry was born in Africa, travelled the world with the merchant navy and now lives in London.

Nicola Tyrer is a journalist and author of the highly acclaimed, *They fought in the Fields*. She lives in Kent with her family.

CHILD OF HAPPY VALLEY
A Memoir

Juanita Carberry spent her childhood in the 1920s and 1930s on a beautiful Kenyan coffee farm. Brought up by black servants and white governesses, much of her time was spent riding and with the tamed wild animals on the estate. This was the White Mischief era, when parents were busy partying and children lived their own hidden lives. But the less innocent adult life began to encroach on her African idyll. At fifteen Juanita became involved in the Lord Erroll affair: she is the only person to whom Delves Broughton confessed to the murder of Lord Erroll. Juanita's story reveals the darkness behind glittering White Mischief society.

For Nellie and Maxwell Trench

'A land where the outcrowded and heavily burdened taxpayer of the older civilisation may seek a more simple yet brighter life.'

Alfred Anderson, author of
Our Newest Colony.
East African Standard Press, 1910

Prologue: My Africa

I have no conventional religious belief but I have a deep respect for destiny. Had the fates decided I was going to grow up a slut or a monster they could not have found a more fertile nursery than Seremai, my childhood home in the White Highlands of Kenya. For I grew up in *White Mischief* country, where the bad boys and girls of some of Britain's most respected titled families gathered to pursue a life of uninhibited pleasure far from the censorious eyes of their disapproving elders back home.

My father John Carberry was a renegade Irish peer who admired Hitler and had sadistic tastes. My stepmother June, famous in the colony for her cheerful promiscuity and prodigious drinking, was an enthusiastic member of the Happy Valley set. Colonials found children a bore. I was referred to as 'the brat' or, if I was caught listening to grown-up conversation, 'sod ears'.

Happily the Fates decided that, despite my origins, I should grow up my own person. What June Carberry and her friends missed out on, as they flirted, got drunk and shouted at the servants, was the uniqueness of Africa. For all they got out of it they might as well have been in Surrey.

Those of us who grew up there can never rid our souls of its bewitching imprint, no matter where we live now. I only have to hear the call

1

of a hyena or the mysterious mewing cry o
the great fish eagle in a television wildlife
programme to feel my throat tighten with
homesickness.

My childhood was spent in the majestic
primitive Africa of before the war; a wild
mysterious land, which man shared with the
greatest profusion of wildlife any continent can
offer. I am aware, as I see it all — people,
animals, landscape — being ravaged by the
onward march of tarmac and consumerism, that
I was privileged to know it as it was.

My friends were never the brash, suburban
types who came to my stepmother's parties.
They were the decent hard-working colonial
families, who outnumbered the Happy Valley
types by a hundred to one and whose vision built
the roads, the hotels, the hospitals, the
racecourses, the clubs and the shops they took
for granted. They were the Africans, whose
language I spoke from childhood; industrious,
sunny-natured and extraordinarily tolerant of
their demanding and often selfish masters.

At the age of fifteen I became involved in the
murder of Lord Erroll, the uncrowned king of
the Happy Valley set. The realisation that her
testimony risked sending the man accused of
murdering him to the gallows gave 'the brat' a
new status. What we who lived it didn't know
was that we were the last chapter of colonial
history and that never again, in the words of
Harold Macmillan, would we have it so good.

1

He Who Is Not Taught by His Mother
Will Be Taught by the World

(Kikuyu saying)

I was not an orphan in the literal sense, yet there
was no organic involvement with parents in the
way most people expect from close blood ties. In
an unusual symmetry both my mother and my
father had been dead for several years before
anyone told me. And the discovery, in both
cases, was an accident.

It might seem strange to people reading this
today that I hadn't noticed that my mother
wasn't around, but this was colonial Africa in the
Twenties. Children and adults led separate lives
and dined at separate tables. It was the era of
nursery wings, when nannies and governesses
were employed with the specific brief of keeping
tiresome children out of the way so that adults
could continue their life of pleasure uninter-
rupted.

My cousin Robin blew the gaff on my
mother's death. We were both about six and we
had a quarrel. We were staying at Granny's house
in Nairobi and were picking violets for her. I
taunted her, the way children do: 'I'll tell my
mother on you.'

'No, you won't.'

'Yes, I will.'

'No you won't,' countered Robin. 'You can't. 'Cos she's dead. So there.'

My mother was Maïa Anderson, a second-generation settler who had spent most of her life in Africa. I was only three when she died, but in those three years, while I'd remained at the family home in Kenya in the charge of an English nanny, she'd spent months at a time travelling, visiting the United States, where she and my father had planned to emigrate, and England, where she had learned to fly the year before she died. My mother became a pioneering airwoman in the early daredevil days of civil aviation and was the first person to fly from Mombasa to Nairobi. Just weeks after her pioneering flight she was killed at Nairobi airfield in front of a crowd of horrified onlookers, one of whom was the husband who had introduced her to the sport.

As in the old fairy tales, for me it was the kind parent who died, while the nasty one survived. My mother, who was known to everyone as Bubbles because of her lively personality, was universally liked by her wide circle of friends. The handwritten notes in the dilapidated green-backed exercise book that she used as a baby record book, which I still have, suggest that she was delighted with her baby daughter, although a little uncertain what to christen her. The first two pages are devoted to a poem addressed to me, touching in its childishness and even written in a childish hand — but she was only twenty-one at the time.

4

Virginia's love is serene and true,
Jane's is a motherly tending.
Starry is flashing,
Passionate, dashing:
A blaze of longing to give, to do,
A life of breaking and mending.
Which would you choose if it lay with you?
Virginia?
        Starry?
                Jane?

In the end, the choice was an amalgam: Juanita
Virginia Sistare Carberry. Juanita is the nearest
Spanish will get to 'little Jane' and Sistare, while
sounding like the flashing, dashing 'starry' which
so appealed to her, was also a compliment to a
relative on the Carberry side.

My mother disappears early from this story. I
have no memory of her and feel I can assess her
dispassionately. In many ways she was ahead of
her time. Her courage, her conviction that you
can do whatever you want to do, irrespective of
your sex, put into practice at a time when other
colonial wives seem to have been mere social
butterflies, makes me wish I'd known her.

I, of course, only knew my father and the
emotion he aroused in me was fear. He was a
tall, athletically built man with distinctive
narrow-set eyes of a piercing ocean blue. I was
afraid of those eyes, which always seemed to be
boring into my heart, looking for evidence of
wrongdoing. But more than the eyes I feared his
voice, the barking way he had of pronouncing my
name, with the emphasis on the last syllable,

5

'Juanita'. Whenever I heard that call, sitting alone, in classic only-child mode, in my avocado tree, my blood would freeze. 'What have I done now? Will it mean a beating?' I would think in terror. Ironic, then, that it was my father who was to bring me up.

★   ★   ★

My father was John Carberry. In reality he was Lord Carberry, the tenth baron and sixth baronet (and because of this I am entitled to style myself the Honourable Juanita Carberry). He spent his childhood in a Gothic — and Gothically named — castle in Ireland, Castle Freke. Of all Eire's numerous ruined once-grand country houses, Castle Freke is one of the grandest and certainly the weirdest. For generations, the house, with its 1000 acres of prime farming country, had been the seat of the Barons Carberry, who owed their lands to the regicide Oliver Cromwell.

Castle Freke today is a creepy place but, in view of the tortured nature of the feuds, hatreds and plottings its echoing rooms have been witness to, maybe this is not surprising. The stone walls stand open to the soft but relentless curtains of grey rain that sweep in for much of the year from the Atlantic in rhythmic airborne waves. The endless vista of glassless stone casements stare blackly out from the stone façade like empty eye sockets in a giant skull. Yet this was no medieval fortress abandoned centuries ago for the softer comforts of modernity. Its ruinous state is the direct result of a bitter feud between John Carberry and his mother Mary, my grandmother. The row was never resolved and has acted like a curse, festering down the decades and casting a shadow over my childhood. The Africans believe that places have spirits — *shaitani* — which must be respected or they become mean and vengeful. Did the *shaitani* of Castle Freke have it in for my family?

In the early years of the twentieth century, when my father was a child — addressed as 'Your Lordship' by the retainers, tended by servants who still believed in the Little People and surrounded by peasant women whose second sight enabled them to foretell death — the house buzzed with life and was the acme of fashion and elegance. There were balls and dinners for the local gentry, the hunt met regularly there, while the numberless bedrooms were always filled with parties of guests from all over Ireland and from England. Jo, John Carberry's daughter by his first marriage, remembers the strange stilted life she led, as a pampered aristocratic toddler, at Castle Freke. She had not one but two starchily uniformed nannies to look after her. Their daily task was to place her, swaddled against the cold in ermine tails, in a small dogcart pulled by a Shetland pony and conduct her down to the beach to benefit from the bracing sea air. A large plaid blanket would be spread on the sand and she would be placed in the middle of it and admonished to sit still. One of the things she remembers about Castle Freke in its intact state was that in the room known as the saloon, which measured seventy-five by thirty feet, there was a full-sized stuffed elephant.

John Carberry lived amid this epic splendour until 1913 when his mother, Mary Carberry, gave a grand ball to celebrate her elder son and heir's coming of age. All the quality in Cork and the tenants on the estate were invited. The fare included 'several hundred buns' supplied by the local baker and a 'horse-load' of beer and porter brought from the neighbouring town of Clonakilty.

Hot on the heels of this ball my father launched his bombshell. He announced that he would be turning his mother out of Castle Freke, not because he wanted it for himself, but because he was putting it on the market. For good measure he threw in that he intended to discard the title and to emigrate.

The news must have rocked Ireland like an earthquake. To bite the hand that fed, when it was, as in the case of Mary, Lady Carberry, soft and white, and covered with jewels, was unheard of. What, peasants and gentry must have wondered, happened to *noblesse oblige*?

What must my grandmother — who, through marrying into the Carberry dynasty, had become one of the grandest ladies in Irish society — have felt at this embarrassingly public rejection of herself by her eldest son? And what lay behind it?

Mary Carberry was a complex woman. She was an intelligent and articulate writer, who published several books. In her diaries, letters

and poems there are many affectionate refer-
ences to my father. He seems to have been a
lively, intelligent child and the anecdotes she
relates suggest that, at least while he was small,
they shared a close, loving relationship. In one
letter to her parents' home in Hertfordshire,
Mary, describing night-time alone with her two
children in Castle Freke after her husband's
untimely death at the age of thirty, writes: 'John,
half-waking in his little bed beside mine, puts
out his little hand to find mine, and so we fall
asleep.'

But Mary Carberry could also be a tough
customer and was regarded by her immediate
family as a highly acquisitive woman and a snob.
Having herself married considerably above her
station, it is said that in her crusade to improve
the family fortunes she persuaded one of her
sisters to marry a duke, even though she knew he
had syphilis. She was unfailingly unpleasant to
John Carberry's first wife José Metcalfe whom,
as a commoner and an Australian, she
considered socially inferior to the daughter of an
old landed family she would have selected as a
daughter-in-law. José said that whenever she and
John visited Castle Freke Mary Carberry had all
the family heirlooms hidden away lest John claim
them which, as his father's heir, he was fully
entitled to do. No one ever seemed to call when
José was staying. She found out later that her
mother-in-law told her neighbours that José
didn't want to be bothered with callers, which
was a complete fabrication.

In later life my father sought to explain his

pathological dislike of his mother — whom he christened 'bloody Mary' — by insisting that she was a hypocrite, who presented a façade of piety and good works while being consumed by snobbery and deceit. He claimed to have caught her in a compromising situation with Christopher Sandford (known as Kit), an eye surgeon from Cork, whom she later married. No one is sure whether this occurred when Algy, her first husband, was still alive or during the period when, as far as the outside world was concerned, Mary was in mourning. John was only six when his father died in 1898 and it seems unlikely that a child of this age would have realised the significance of what he had interrupted. It is more likely, therefore, that John surprised the lovers some time during the years between the ninth Lord Carberry's death and my grandmother's marriage to Kit Sandford in 1902.

If John Carberry drew an unflattering picture of his mother, the one he painted of himself as a child was hardly more genial. Although he spoke little of his past, he enjoyed recounting a story dating back to his early childhood, which ridiculed his mother's doomed attempts to teach him the virtues of gentleness. According to him, on his fourth Christmas she said to him, 'Today is Christmas Day and I want you to be especially kind to animals, particularly the cat.' He returned to her some time later with the announcement, 'I've given the cat all the canaries to eat.' As a teenager he went to stay with his grandparents and aunts at their house near St Albans, which had its own home farm.

On arrival, he produced some darts, which he proceeded to throw at a sheep. Because of the thickness of the fleece the animal did not suffer but the family, who all adored animals, were horrified. The next day the pig was heard squealing and was found to have a dart embedded in its flesh. When John Carberry was made, by his furious grandfather, to give the cowman a shilling for removing the dart he was indignant, retorting that it would have been fairer 'if you would give me a shilling for having such a good aim'. Far from expressing contrition, John positively gloated over the sticking. At the end of his thank-you letter to his grandfather he added a drawing of a pig with, in the air, a dart winging towards it.

He even tried to kill his younger brother — Granny found Ralfe hanging in terror from the stone sill of one of the upper windows at Castle Freke while John pounded his hands with a rock to make him let go. Ralfe never forgot the incident and went so far as to warn his son Peter, the present Lord Carberry, who is my cousin, not to go out and visit my father in Kenya and specifically never to fly with him. He was convinced he would try to push him out of the plane. The idea of killing fascinated John Carberry. He once startled Peter Carberry's stepmother, a pleasant, ascetic sort of woman, by asking whether there was anyone she wanted 'bumping off'. If she did, she was to let him know and he would 'turn them upside down in a plane over the jungle'. There is no doubt that John Carberry loved to shock and he cared little for the opinion of others. Mary Lovell, biographer of the aviator Beryl Markham, wrote of my father, 'He was an unpleasant character with a cruel sadistic streak, particularly towards animals. During nearly 100 interviews conducted for this book not one person could find a good word to say for him.' This, then, was the man who was to bring me up.

★ ★ ★

My mother's background was much less bizarre and produced a gentler character. She was born on 20 January 1904 in Bristol and came out to Kenya when she was a baby. When she was old enough she was sent to board at the Maison St Pierre in Ghent in Belgium, the school her mother had attended. Somewhat dramatically, she was trapped there when war was declared in August 1914. Her eldest brother Gerald, who was studying to be a doctor at the Royal College of Medicine in London, was ordered to rescue her and only just made it back before the fighting began. He brought her to England where she spent the rest of the war with him and his wife Caroline. She was not to see Africa again for six long years, returning home with them at the age of sixteen in 1920 which, coincidentally, was the year John Carberry took the extraordinary and unheard-of step of relinquishing his title and changing his name by deed poll from Lord Carberry with one 'r' to plain Mister John Carberry with two 'r's.

Kenyan society in the early decades of the

12

century was a small, tightly knit group of people. My mother's parents were now Mayor and Mayoress of Nairobi and it cannot have been long before their only daughter and John Carberry met on the social circuit.

John Carberry liked his women beautiful. He had been married and divorced by the time he met my mother. His first wife had been a glamorous Australian blonde called José Metcalfe. Perhaps now it was time for a brunette. Photographs of my mother at this age depict a head-turningly good-looking young woman, with glossy brown hair, centre-parted and fashionably Marcel-waved, a mischievous smile and heavy-lidded languorous hazel eyes. Several of the many press photographs of her that have survived show her in flying gear, yet the way she dressed remained uncompromisingly feminine. Her flying helmet, flatteringly fur-trimmed, sets off the delicacy of her face, there are always pearls round the slender neck and even her leather flying coat is cropped at the knee to show off shapely legs and feet clad in the fashionable strappy shoes of the period.

In January 1922 my mother and John Carberry were married. Maïa was an innocent eighteen-year-old from a hard-working pioneer family. Carberry was a thirty-year-old divorcé who had been brought up to expect deference and unquestioning obedience from all who surrounded him. The difference in age and culture do not appear to have rung any alarm bells. In the eyes of my mother's family John Carberry, with his patrician looks and two-hundred-year-old pedigree, was a catch. Had they known a bit more about him — his strange, tormented childhood, his bitter feud with his mother and in particular his attitude to pregnancy and children — they might have been a bit more cautious.

As in most marriages, there seems to have been a degree of excitement at the beginning. My cousin Peter Anderson often went to Seremai, our house in Nyeri, as a small child and on one occasion was somewhat disconcerted — the way children are by ungainly displays of adult horesplay — to find John chasing a squeaking Maïa round and round the house. But Carberry's response to the news that Maïa was pregnant must have disillusioned her. His reaction was to propose a long ride out into the bush on mules, the idea being that the jogging stride of the animal would dislodge the baby. Maïa told her horrified family that she dared not complain, because of Carberry's hatred of cowardice, and rode on until she fell off her mount. The discomfort was so great that in order not to groan aloud she had literally to bite the dust. Little did she know that history was repeating itself and that my father had tried to abort the baby his first wife, José, was carrying in circumstances if anything even more horrific.

(My father's reaction when José told him she was pregnant was to suggest an abortion. She refused and insisted on returning to Europe for the birth. Most men would have given in at this stage. Not he. He travelled with her on the steamer and tried to persuade the ship's doctor

14

to abort her. When he refused, Carberry insisted he would take her ashore when they reached Port Said, where he knew someone who would oblige him. The horrified doctor warned José not to leave the ship and ended up hiding her in the crew's quarters till they left port.)

John and Maïa Carberry did have one thing in common: both were ahead of their time. Born in the last decade of Queen Victoria's reign, John Carberry was enormously excited by the fast-moving technology of the new age. He loved the liberating methods of travel that came with the dawn of the twentieth century — fast cars and aeroplanes were his passion — and was attracted to any pursuit which involved speed and daring. A man who pushed himself to take risks, he was hugely intolerant of the less brave, branding them contemptuously as cowards. Much of the bullying I was to undergo at his hands has been put down to his well-documented contempt of cowardice.

John Carberry had been flying his own plane since before the First World War. In July 1914, less than a month before its outbreak, he amazed the Irish by becoming the first man to land a plane in Ireland. He took off from a playing field in Cork and landed in Clonakilty twenty minutes later. A week after that he gave another demonstration at the same playing field, this time taking a succession of passengers up with him and indulging in a characteristically daredevil display of looping the loop to, according to press reports, 'shrieks and gasps of terror' from the onlookers. It was, said one of the papers, shortly after this performance that 'the tenth Earl decided to sell his property, renounce his title and emigrate to Kenya'.

Maïa, my mother, was the embodiment of the try-anything post-war emancipated young woman and loved driving. A British newspaper report of the late Twenties describes her as an 'enthusiastic motorist . . . generally to be seen in public only in fleeting glimpses, as she flashes past at the wheel of an up-to-date motor car'. From motoring to flying was just a short hop and Carberry wasted little time in encouraging his new wife to take up his great passion.

In the summer of 1927, two years after my birth, he and Maïa left Kenya for England and their London base, which was a first-floor flat in Jermyn Street in London's West End, just round the corner from the Piccadilly pied-à-terre where Mrs Keppel, the mistress of King Edward VII, used to receive her Royal lover. The purpose of the trip was for my mother to win her pilot's licence. My parents used to drive over to Stag Lane aerodrome in Hendon, the leading civilian airfield of the day, where Carberry would watch while Maïa was put through her paces by instructors from the De Havilland School of Flying. To his undoubted approval Maïa evinced no fear, volunteering to fly at 7000 feet, when to qualify she needed to fly at only 6000, and passing flight, landing and altitude tests within a fortnight. An item in the *Daily Mail* on 8 September 1927 records that Mrs M. Carberry 'completed her tests at Stag Lane Aerodrome, (Edgware) yesterday for her pilot's certificate by ascending 7000 feet in a Moth aeroplane'. The *Sphere* of 10 September 1927 noted, 'Mrs Carberry ... has just completed her tests at Hendon for her pilot's certificate and is shortly to return to her home in Kenya Colony with a Moth aeroplane, the gift of her husband who was a pioneer airman so long ago as 1912.'

Less than a fortnight later Maïa took part in her first international air race. The fact that she was a woman pilot, and delightfully photogenic as well, made her irresistible to the press. On 10 January 1927, as she was starting her journey home, Maïa explained to the air correspondent of the *Daily Chronicle* how owning a plane was going to revolutionise her life in Africa.

As she left England on an Imperial Airways aircraft bound for Paris on her way home to Kenya she said: 'I have bought a little Moth light aeroplane for my own personal use. My husband already owns two planes and flies constantly here and there about the colony.

'By air, from where we live, we can reach Nairobi, the capital, in about 40 minutes flying. If we went by train it would take nine hours. I intend to use my little air-car for shopping trips in the morning into Nairobi, or to see the races, or to attend local amusements. By road transport such a trip would occupy two or three days.

'One of the great comforts to those overseas who possess an aeroplane is that it provides a means of summoning a doctor without delay, in the case of any sudden illness.'

Maïa delighted English journalists with her 'doesn't everyone?' attitude to flying, but her more serious intention was to raise the profile of civilian flying, not as a rich man's sport but because, as she realised, it was the way forward. As she told the *Manchester Guardian* in her impromptu press conference at the airport: 'We shall use our air fleet for the benefit of our neighbours and our great wish is to make the colony air-minded.'

Peter Carberry, however, remembers Maïa as an unhappy figure. As a quite young child he visited her in the Jermyn Street flat, where she was waiting for John Carberry to join her on his return from some overseas flying trip. She brought Peter with her to Stag Lane aerodrome on the day her husband was due to arrive, and took him up in a plane to while away the time. They waited all day but Carberry never appeared and they returned to Jermyn Street without him. Peter recalls Maïa bursting into floods of tears of disappointment.

Temperamentally, Carberry and Maïa were very different, a fact which must have begun to emerge quite early in their relationship. Maïa may have been plucky and adventurous but she was also kind and gentle and would doubtless have been repelled by his cruelty. A story told me by my cousin Patty illustrates Maïa's sensitivity. One night, everyone was at Maxwell Trench's house (Trench was John Carberry's partner and ran the coffee plantation). The adults were playing tennis and people were standing around while the kitchen boy was killing a chicken for supper. Maïa felt it would upset me to see the chicken killed, so she picked me up and walked off to where we were out of sight and earshot of the slaughter, and sat me on her lap till it was all over.

I don't know if my mother missed me when she was in Europe, but she did tell one journalist that while other children had pedal cars her three-year-old daughter 'is in the fashion with her own toy pedal plane'.

In February 1928, three months before my third birthday, my mother came home and immediately set herself the challenge of becoming the first person to fly non-stop from Mombasa to Nairobi. She accomplished the journey in three and a half hours on Thursday, 16 February 1928, bringing the first Coast–Highland air mail with her and arriving to a hero's welcome. She was accompanied by a human passenger, Captain Kenealy, and a tortoise with a pink ribbon tied round its neck, which had been presented to her at Mombasa as a lucky mascot. A vivid description appeared in the *East African Standard* of the rapturous reception given Miss Propaganda — both on the ground and in the air — as the little Moth made its dramatic appearance over the crowds assembled at Ngong airport. With unconscious irony the paper trumpeted that the 'epoch-making journey' was 'an added demonstration of the safety of flight in the Tropics'.

Just over two weeks later my mother was dead. Miss Propoganda, the same plane in which she had so recently made her triumphant pioneering flight, went into a nosedive and plunged to the ground in front of dozens of spectators. The accident happened at Nairobi's Ngong airport, scene of her recent rapturous reception, where she had spent the afternoon at Kenya's first air fair, enjoying tea in the large marquee, serenaded by the King's African Rifles and taking friends up for flights. Maïa companion, Dudley Cowie, a young man whom she was teaching to fly using the facility of the Moth's dual controls, was also killed. My mother was twenty-four, her passenger, twenty-two.

My mother's family believed John Carberry killed Maïa. There had been a clash between them over the fateful flight. Maïa thought she was psychic and had a premonition that it would end in disaster. My cousin Patty, who was about eight at the time, remembers Maïa's growing agitation about the forthcoming display. She says that in the days before her last flight Maïa spoke to her mother and brother (Patty's father Gerald) about her desire to give up flying as she felt something was going to happen. She finally approached Carberry who, characteristically, ridiculed her fear and pooh-poohed her premonition. Dudley, the man who died, didn't want to go up either, not being particularly brave. But Carberry steamrollered everyone.

The cause of the accident was never established. Newspaper reports describe the plane as circling to descend at a height of 500 feet when it appeared to lose speed, began to spin and dived to earth with a horrifying crash.

Witnesses say that Dudley panicked, pulled the joystick into the dive position and then froze so that my mother could not right the plane in time. There is conflicting evidence as to when Maïa died. Some reports say she was thrown or jumped from the plane before it struck the ground and was killed instantly; others that she died about an hour later. The source of my information is my grandmother's scrapbook, a tan morocco-bound exercise book filled with now yellowing pages, in which she faithfully chronicled all newspaper reports featuring her beloved only daughter. Where reference is made to Maïa being alive until after the accident grandmother has underlined the words 'she was alive' and written beside it 'incorrect. It was instantaneous.' Whether to contemplate the thought of a daughter suffering like this was too unbearable or whether the journalist had genuinely made a mistake I shall never know.

The accident stunned the colony, not just because my mother was pretty and popular, but because her energetic and intrepid youth symbolised the new era — one in which the pompous fuddy-duddies of nineteenth-century colonialism were being ousted by a confident new generation at ease with the latest technology and eager to sweep East Africa into a modernising new age.

My mother was laid to rest in a grave filled with golden shower, a flamboyant tropical climber with eye-catching orange flowers. She was buried with her flying kit. Before the coffin was lowered into the grave John Carberry placed on it part of the

21

broken propeller of her aeroplane.

Obituaries appeared all round the world. The *Irish Times*, the *Bystander*, the *Daily Mirror*, the *Sketch*, the *News of the World*, the *Daily Mail*, *The Times*, the *Telegraph*, the *Star* and the *Morning Post* all carried reports giving her her title: 'Peeress Killed In a Flight', 'Lady Carberry killed in Husband's Presence', 'Peeress's Death Jump From Falling Plane'. All were faithfully pasted into my grandmother's cuttings book.

I have been told that John Carberry was devastated by my mother's death. Perhaps guilt played a part in his grief and he did feel it was his fault. After the accident he went to his in-laws' house in Nairobi and my cousins were ordered not to come into the sitting-room because he was in there, weeping.

Among the Andersons the feeling was that by the time of the accident Maïa had been feeling disillusioned and neglected. John Carberry was never one to let any of his wives stand in the way of his amusements. Throughout his marriage to Maïa, and throughout my childhood, he was continually away on leisure or business trips. Patty remembers my mother spending a lot of her time staying at Granny's home in Nairobi, which is hardly the behaviour of a fulfilled wife. It was even said that she had sought consolation in the arms of another and that I might not be John Carberry's child.

2

A Taste of Termites

Seremai was the name of my childhood home perched more than 6000 feet above sea level in Kenya's magnificent White Highlands. The word has a lush, exotic feel to it, evoking visions of dusky maidens and palm-fringed beaches. In fact, it is a Masai word meaning 'place of death' and is said to commemorate a battle between them and the local Kikuyu tribe. John Carberry acquired 650 acres of this land on 17 April 1915 and built the house in the later years of the First World War. Five miles from the town of Nyeri, just over a hundred from Nairobi, it was the centre of a substantial estate dedicated to the making of money. Carberry was a tireless entrepreneur whose obsession with money was intensified by the desire to prove to his mother that he could become rich without recourse to inherited wealth. After the acrimonious parting Mary Carberry had used the law in a way that now seems highly dubious to ensure that her eldest son never inherited the Carberry capital or the extremely valuable family silver and works of art. In Africa he set out to build a fresh fortune of his own. He succeeded. By the time I came along he was a wealthy man.

I should explain why I refer to my father as John Carberry. From the very beginning our bonding mechanism was faulty. He never behaved as a father towards me and so I never responded as a daughter to him. I can't recall him ever touching me — not a squeeze or even a peck on the cheek. I certainly don't remember in all the years I lived with him glimpsing any hint of affection for me. Where other fathers give their children nicknames imbued with tenderness, I was 'the brat' or 'sod ears'. And he, to me, was 'JC'. As I grew older and my behaviour began more often to rouse the violent predator that lurked in his dark soul, ever watchful for the chance to pounce on the helpless, I came to dread the barked 'Juanita' that signalled his displeasure.

JC spent a great deal of his time away from Seremai — flying continued to be a major passion right up to the outbreak of the Second World War — but he also did a lot of travelling for pleasure, to London and America in particular. It is doubtless because of this that my early childhood memories are of a life filled with affection, sunshine and freedom of a kind modern children can only dream of. I didn't go to school until I was seven and although desultory attempts were made during those years to make me literate and numerate, my memories are chiefly of playing in a magnificent landscape populated by my favourite companions — animals.

My childhood home was only thirty miles south of the Equator. I am a tropical creature. I love warmth and the freedom a warm climate brings — wearing the minimum of clothing and going barefoot. To this day I dislike wearing shoes and never wear them indoors. Europeans tend to imagine Africa as excessively hot or enervatingly humid. The climate in the Highlands is more like a warmer, drier version of English weather, which is why English settlers felt so at home there. The heat was never oppressive. We didn't need to sleep under mosquito nets the way they had to down at the coast because there were no mosquitoes. The sun shone most days except during the rains, but, because of the altitude, mornings and evenings were cool, so much so that we usually had an open fire in the drawing-room at night.

Throughout my childhood I took it for granted that the great golden sun rises in a cloudless sky at 6 a.m. and that by 7 p.m. — there is no twilight in the tropics — it would be completely dark. Each day from our veranda I savoured what must be one of the most exhilarating views in the world. Daybreak in the Highlands, before the heat had blanketed the landscape in a blurry haze, was a marvel of clarity and brilliance. If I looked to the right I could see the twin peaks of Mount Kenya, which lay about thirty miles north-east of us as the crow flies, towering 17,000 feet above the surrounding landscape and, despite the baking heat, permanently snowcapped for the last 3000 feet. If I looked left my eye took in the thickly forested green hump of Nyeri Hill.

Seremai was five miles from the township of Nyeri if you took the main road which ran between Nanyuki and Nyeri, crossing the Chania river. There was also a short cut which we often used. This led down a bumpy rough murram track (murram is a reddish grit used for surfacing minor roads in the colonial era) and meant crossing the river by a makeshift wooden bridge. In the rains it became impossible as the river rose and you couldn't be sure the bridge would hold because the Africans regularly removed bits of it for firewood. Many roads became well-nigh impassable to cars during the rains, much to the frustration of European drivers who feared the ravages unseen obstructions might wreak on their undercarriage. A familiar sight during the rains in the old days before the roads were properly surfaced was a car driving along up to its axles in water with an African walking in front carrying a stick to check for pot-holes. If JC found himself in this situation with no African I would be kicked out into the flood to do the job.

A curiosity which I only ever remember on the hilly winding roads of Nyeri was that running parallel to the proper road, like an early version of the dual carriageway, there was often another track known as a *ngombe* track. This was for the use of the ox wagons. In the rainy season the wheels of the ox carts gouged deep ruts in the sodden murram surface and the idea of the *ngombe* track was to keep the carts off the car road during the rains. As these tracks never had any traffic on them, in later years I used to ride along them on my pony.

As you left the Nyeri — Nanyuki road and entered the estate, immediately on your right was the hangar where JC housed his planes and in front of it his private airstrip. When war broke out in 1939 the government put tree trunks across the airstrip to prevent the Italians, who were the colonial masters of neighbouring Somaliland and allied with Hitler against Britain, from landing there. This infuriated JC since it clipped his wings in every sense, but it pleased me as the tree trunks made an ideal jumping course for me and my pony. Beyond the airstrip there was a group of round thatched huts lived in by Africans who worked on the coffee farm. African lore dictates that if someone dies in a hut it must be burned and I remember this happening on one occasion, probably as a result of leprosy, which was still rife among the Africans then. More often than not, they didn't want to burn their homes. In these cases the victim would be dragged out to die outside the hut. The hyenas sometimes helped.

The coffee trees on which the estate's wealth was founded were in plots bounded by murram avenues planted with grevillea trees. Grevilleas, which are known in South Africa as silver oak, used to be grown all over the Highlands to provide shade for the coffee, though now their distinctive mottled timber is increasingly used in cabinet making. They are magnificent trees, with delicate fern-like leaves, dark green on top, silvery underneath with flamboyant orange blooms up to twelve centimetres in length similar in shape to a bottle brush flower. These literally drip nectar and are a magnet, not just for bees but for a whole variety of the jewel-bright nectar-feeding sunbirds that abound in the Highlands.

One of these grevillea avenues led to the house itself. For the last 200 or 300 yards jacaranda trees had been planted inside the grevilleas. The jacaranda is an up-country plant. Its showy mauvey blue bell-shaped blooms, which grow to four centimetres in length, make it one of Africa's most beguiling flowers. Because the jacarandas were inside the grevilleas they leaned towards each other, and when the petals dropped they made a carpet of blue underfoot so that as you approached the house when the jacarandas were in bloom it was through a tunnel of blue blossoms.

As you drove through the jacaranda tunnel you came out in front of a vast horseshoe-shaped lawn, which was never green except during the rains, in the midst of which was an immense monkey puzzle tree. To reach the house you turned down the right side of the lawn where the circular drive encompassed a large flower bed planted with long-legged blue and white agapanthus lilies. Beyond the drive was the tennis court, made of murram like the drive (I never knew grass courts existed until I came to Europe). In my mother's day tennis parties had been a regular feature of social life at Seremai but JC didn't play and I don't remember it being used much.

Our home was a one-storey grey stone building. Like so many colonial houses it boasted no particular architectural distinction. It had a raised pyramid-shaped roof made of cedar bark shingles, tall chimneys for the open fires and a raised veranda on two sides.

The house was built round a paved courtyard in the middle of which was a raised flower bed. This covered the cesspit and was planted with pink oleander bushes and gorgeous croton lilies, which flowered each year in the rains. Once the cesspit had to be dug up because two of the mongooses that we kept as pets had tunnelled into it, on the look-out for insects and snakes, and had fallen in. Their whereabouts were not discovered until we missed them at bedtime and went calling for them, only to hear their grateful answering chirrup issuing from the cesspit.

The courtyard at Seremai was surrounded by a corridor and the rooms of the house led off from this. My favourite was the drawing-room. It had a beautiful parquet floor, made of cedar wood, which was kept immaculately polished, a baronial fireplace and a grand piano, which must have been put there to impress as it was hardly ever used. John Carberry, like most settlers of that era, was a dedicated hunter (he was described in my mother's obituary in the *Star* as 'one of the greatest big-game shots in the world') and the drawing-room was filled with his hunting trophies. A huge buffalo's head dominated the fireplace; one of the sofas was covered with a black leopard skin, while a lamp made of a stuffed albino colobus monkey holding up a light bulb stood on the piano.

Leading out of the drawing-room was the dining-room. This contained the gun cupboard. It was never locked. As far as Europeans were concerned, Africa was a wild place. Everyone had guns, for shooting game and for protection. The adults always had one to hand at night, either on the bedside table or under the pillow. Women had pretty little pistols inlaid with mother-of-pearl. Maxwell Trench, my father's business partner at Seremai, taught me to shoot when I was quite young with the .22 rifle that had belonged to my mother. We often went out into the bush to shoot a 'Tommy' (Thomson's gazelle) for the pot. It was delicious, tasting like venison. Maxwell taught me as an absolute golden rule never, *ever*, to point a gun at anyone. 'Don't give me that crap about 'why, it's not even loaded',' he would say. 'If anyone tells you that, never take it on trust. Always open the breech and check.'

On one side of the drawing-room was the kitchen block. This wing included the pantry and laundry, and also the bedroom and bathroom of Monsieur Beaudet, a kindly Frenchman kept permanently on the payroll to maintain John Carberry's fleet of aeroplanes. On the other side the corridor led on from the drawing-room to a series of guest-rooms ending with John Carberry's bedroom and luxurious *en suite* bathroom. Tacked on to this — and suitably distanced from the rooms where the adults entertained — was what had been built as a nursery extension. This comprised the sun parlour, two bedrooms and a bathroom for me and whoever was employed to look after me. The fact that my bedroom was so isolated from the hub of the household was to make it, in later years, an ideal prison when, as punishment for an assortment of alleged breaches of discipline, I would be locked up without regular meals, sometimes for days on end.

When I think of Seremai, more than the house it is the outside I remember: the jewel-bright colours of tropical blossoms — purple bougainvillaea romping up everything from the tennis court fence to the gum trees, lush hibiscus in every shade in the paintbox, the vibrant yellowy orange of the tropical climber Golden Shower, the brick-red tulip-shaped flowers of the flame trees. What makes life in the tropics so delightful is the feeling that the life force has been turned up a notch, like a TV set whose colour button has been slightly over-adjusted. Because of the long hours of sunlight the plants are bigger, brighter, more exuberantly scented than in temperate climes. I remember, too, the chatters, grunts and whoops of the wildlife and that inimitable smell that evokes Africa so powerfully to those who know it intimately — the invigorating, pungent, smell released by the thirsty African soil as it gulps down the first life-restoring drops of the longed-for rains.

I spent most of my childhood out of doors. The adults, with their endless drinking and the raucous joviality that it invariably induced, repelled me. I preferred the company of the Africans, who were noisy too, but in a spontaneous, good-humoured way that drew you to them. Much of the din in Africa, however, came from the never-ending battle for survival in which the teeming local wildlife were either exulting aggressors or protesting victims. Kites soared high above, mewing like seagulls, their restless eyes drilling down for a chick separated from its mother. Chickens ran free at Seremai, providing us with eggs and delicious, fragrant meat. At the sound of the mewing the hen would utter a harsh warning call which instantly sent the chicks dashing for cover. Kites also take mongooses. Mongooses are very noisy and rush about chirruping. As a kite appeared overhead one mongoose would give a warning growl and all the others would vanish. United in danger, the animals learned to understand each other's language. When the mongoose who was acting as scout gave his 'kite's about' warning growl, the chicks would scatter without waiting for instructions from the hen.

Because so many animals in Africa are nocturnal the hours of darkness are, if anything, noisier than the day. In the Highlands the night air is rent with barks, coughs, grunts, growls, shrieks and whoops. In England you might get a cat, or perhaps a fox, trying to get the lid off your dustbin. In Africa it's hyenas. They have a big vocabulary and nothing is more evocative of an African night than the whooping, snarling, yelling and screeching of hyenas as they arrive to raid your dustbin and leave replete. You hear the bark of a jackal — 'brak-brak' — as it calls for a mate, or the one sound that really frightened me: a cross between the sawing of wood and a cough, which told you that a leopard was out there.

The mainstay of life at Seremai, where the rich red earth was super-fertile, was coffee. The whole process, from growing to packaging, took place on site as the estate had its own factory. The coffee bushes, which in 1915 had been tender seedlings a few inches high, were now mature growths, pruned to a height of about six feet to make for easy picking. The cycle of the coffee plant is a colourful and fragrant affair starting with white flowers, smelling of orange blossom, whose blooming is triggered by the rains, and ending as scarlet berries on the laden bushes. When the fruit was ripe the Africans would be sent in to pick the coffee on bushes that stretched as far as the eye could see. Inside every berry are two grooved seeds, lying in a bed of silvery skin. These are the coffee beans. The berries were picked, peeled and thrown into a huge heap. Then they were washed and put on to trays to dry in the sun. After that they were husked and roasted in a large drum with a wood fire underneath. The final stage involved placing the beans in their cellophane-wrapped packages. I loved going down to the factory and helping with the packaging. The specially made wrapping was printed all over with 'C and T Coffee' for Carberry and Trench. The packages were destined for the smartest breakfast tables in faraway England. In those class-conscious days even the coffee came in different qualities. The cheaper type, which the locals liked, was called 'buni', while the blue-chip stuff, which we drank at the house, was the best 'arabica'.

Further on from the coffee factory was the soda water factory. Most of the time the output from here was plain soda water and ginger beer, but at one stage John Carberry imported essence of Coca-Cola from the United States. I thought the result was delicious — even better than milk, which was always my favourite drink — and was very disappointed when he ran into a trade name bar and was forced to cease production.

Sugar cane was another crop grown at Seremai. The Africans used to peel off the waxy heavy skin so that I could chew it and suck out the sticky sweet juice. The fibrous bits that were left I spat out and gave to my pony who loved them. Down at the factory there was a machine for crushing the cane. The juice flowed out through a spout into big barrels. I used to hold a tin under the spout and catch the liquid, which was full of bits — fragments of stem, ants — but I didn't care. It was delicious. Barrels full of crushed sugar juice used to be brought up to both our house and the Trenches' home, and placed either side of the massive wood-burning stoves, known as Dover stoves, which were found in the kitchens of all the Europeans. There they stayed for some time until the juice developed a froth on it. I did not know it at the time, but this was the first stage in the making of rum.

Maxwell Trench, who was the working arm of Carberry and Trench, was a white Jamaican who had come to Kenya in 1914 after a hurricane washed most of the family's coffee estates near Montego Bay into the sea. Like all West Indians, he was an expert on rum. The coffee factory housed a still, which completed the process started courtesy of the Dover stoves. Distilling was permitted provided it was strictly for personal consumption. John Carberry was never one to pass up the chance to make money and was always prepared to cut corners as far as the law was concerned. When tennis parties were held at Seremai, guests were given bottles of rum. Although it was not strictly for sale, they would nevertheless leave generous gratuities to thank Carberry for his trouble. Later on, the still was used for making Crème de Menthe, gin and eau-de-Cologne. The gin, apparently, was not a success.

Life in Africa in the Twenties and Thirties was still fairly primitive, even for rich settlers, and electricity was a problem. The Chania river, which ran through our property at the foot of a steep track punctuated by hairpin bends, was put to work for the new masters. The coffee factory was run on water power. Water was channelled along a conduit (we called it a furrow), which worked a dynamo. Beyond the factory the furrow filled out into a succession of dammed-up pools in which Carberry and Maxwell Trench reared tilapia, a freshwater fish with a delicious flavour that I often had for dinner. The Africans used to trap the fish, which was then driven by Trench's wife Nellie to be sold, along with grapes and tomatoes, which were also grown commercially at Seremai, in the market at Nyeri. Nellie was a tireless worker and in addition looked after the enormous vegetable garden shared by the two households. The perfect climate and rich soil must have made growing crops a delight. We had mangoes, avocados, oranges and lemons, plums, mulberries and every vegetable you can think of, including carrots, cabbages, lettuce, tomatoes, spinach and *kalulu* (Jamaican spinach).

My favourite haunt at Seremai lay at the back of the house, which was reached by taking a left instead of a right as you emerged from the jacaranda tunnel. This area housed mundane features like the water tank, garages, petrol pumps and offices to do with the coffee production. It was also where the animals lived. In those days isolated farms had to be self-sufficient, and the chickens and rabbits were there to provide eggs and meat. Like generations of children who grew up without supermarkets I was fascinated, rather than distressed, by the way a chicken could run around the yard after its head had been cut off — usually with an African in hot pursuit. But not all our animals were destined for the pot. We had a whole variety of pets. I had a black-and-white terrier-sized mongrel called Boppy. We always made sure the dogs were in the house at night, however, to protect them from leopards, who roamed the Highlands in substantial numbers and were particularly partial to dogs. In some cases this partiality even led to humans being attacked as, of course, a dog being pursued runs to its master. When I was young, stories were told of Europeans sitting on their verandas sipping sundowners when suddenly a terrified dog would appear with a leopard close behind it. We also had tortoises. Tortoises in England are usually ancient, invariably solitary and celibate. In Africa they are passionate — and vocal — Casanovas and breed at a prodigious rate. As a child voyeur

36

I relished the grunts of ecstasy uttered by the seemingly insatiable male tortoises.

Chameleons, too, were among my pet creatures. You would find them sitting on bushes. They were easy to catch because they do everything in slow motion — everything, that is, except flicking out their long tongues to catch insects, which they do faster than the eye can follow. Africans are afraid of chameleons. They think they bring bad luck. I used to like frightening the *totos* (African children) with them. Often I would bring one home and put it on a branch in my bedroom and feed it *dudus* (insects). It wasn't interested unless they were alive.

My favourite animals, though, were the cheetahs. The Africans used to catch cheetah cubs and sell them to the Europeans who reared them as pets. At one stage we had five. Three were not domesticated and lived in a big run, but Jackie and Muriel ran free, enjoying the run of the house and would lie on the sofa in the drawing-room like large domestic cats. I adored them and they me.

Cheetahs are highly playful and love to stalk you and then pounce. This is great fun but has its drawbacks, as cheetahs have a retractable dew-claw which they use to trip their prey and hold it down while they eat, and they use this claw when they are playing, jumping out as you walk unsuspectingly past and hooking it into your ankle. Of course, the claw is full of gunge and the wound quickly turns septic, leading to ulcers, or veld sores as we called them, which are common in the tropics. I was forever getting veld sores. We were miles away from medical help and treated these types of problems ourselves. The treatment for veld sores was magnesium sulphate (Epsom salts, in reality) and glycerine mixed to a paste and applied to the wound overnight. It hurt like hell, but it really cleaned it.

In the end the cheetahs were all shut up because they used to terrorise the Africans who worked on the coffee farm, and chased and killed their goats and chickens. They didn't do this because they were particularly bloodthirsty but because it is in the nature of cheetahs to chase anything which flees. Africans feared them because they could not tell them apart from leopards, despite the fact that cheetahs have a spotted coat, while the markings on a leopard are rosette-shaped and leopards are much stockier than cheetahs, who have a distinctive tear-shaped mark on the inside corners of their eyes. Temperamentally they are different too. Leopards are very unreliable and treacherous, whereas cheetahs make friendly and dependable pets. Several people who lived in Africa took on young leopards or lions but it invariably ended in tragedy with the animal needing to be killed or a human life lost. One woman I knew kept a lion which attacked one of my husbands. We managed to rescue him, but the following week the same lion ate the woman's cook and had to be shot.

The cheetahs needed to be fed a diet of raw meat — if you don't give them a natural diet they develop rickets. This meant regular drives out into the bush, usually at night, using a spotlight, to shoot buck, which is how we acquired another pet. Sometimes the buck you shot had a baby, in which case you brought it home and reared it, and it grew up tame. Hans was a reed buck we caught in this way. When he was a baby we had to feed him cow's milk from a baby's bottle. He loved to play rough, lowering his head and charging like a billy-goat. The problem was that a reed buck's horns stick out in front and Hans grew into a very strong animal who was dangerous. First, we tried putting champagne corks on his horns, but he got those off straight away. Then we held him down, cut a thread into his horn and screwed big nuts on to them, but they didn't hold as the horns tapered towards the end. When he was grown-up he used to come to the kitchen door and ask for his bowl of milk, which was given to him in a *sufuria* (saucepan). We had him quite a while and then one day he didn't come back.

We also had a serval cat, whom the boys christened Kibau, who was totally wild and who lived in a big run and, like many other Europeans, a tribe of mongooses. Mongooses make delightful pets. They run around in a pack and are very noisy and social in the day, while at night they curl up and go to sleep like cats. When they meet other members of the pack there is always a terrific ritual greeting. They are extremely clean. If you put down newspaper they will use that as a lavatory, and only that. They are also totally fearless. When they bite it hurts like holy hell and they hang on like terriers — to make them let go you have to jab them on the nose with a lighted cigarette. At Seremai they ran around and bossed all the other animals into submission. If you were at table eating and you dropped a piece of food only one animal would move and that was the mongoose. If a cat was eating a mouse or a bird, the mongoose would creep up and steal it from behind.

I loved the cheetahs dearly but I was also very fond of Bwana Jo, a chimp. When he was small he used to be led around on a dog chain and given to people to cuddle. But then he got stronger and more dangerous, so he was given a longer chain, which ran up and down a wire stretched between two posts. He lived on the large lawn in front of the house. He had his own little house for shade and shelter, and was, I think, fairly happy. I used to get up early, long before the adults who were usually sleeping off a night's drinking, and play and romp with Bwana Jo. It was he who introduced me to the pleasures of eating termites, which look like large flying ants and appear in great numbers during the rains. I used to watch him eating them and had noticed that the Africans ate them too, so one day I decided to try them. I found them delicious. I still do — nice and creamy — but you have to be quick as they do have nippers. Years later, when I was in the army, I was out on a date with a new boyfriend. It was during the rains and the termites were flying round the lights in the bar where we were sitting. As I studied the menu I absent-mindedly caught and ate a termite, the way you might nibble an olive or a crisp. The boyfriend never dated me again. The Africans also eat locusts, which used to come down to Kenya in huge black clouds from their breeding grounds in the Sudan. They fried them in butter. I have tried them, but to me they lack the charm of termites and taste of grass. My friend Bwana Jo had bitten somebody but I had no thought of fear. In my view he and I were best buddies. Then, one day, someone saw me with him and shouted at me to come away from that dangerous animal. That planted in me the seed of fear and mistrust and I never again felt able to go up to him afterwards. It changed him too. Every time I got within range he would lunge aggressively at me.

Of course, there were creatures you learned to be wary of, such as poisonous snakes — we occasionally got cobras and mambas in the house, which would cause total panic, with the Europeans yelling in terror for the Africans to kill the things and the Africans, who are terrified of snakes, throwing sticks and brooms about. You would always give your shoe a shake before putting it on to check no creepy crawly had climbed in. If, like me, you ran barefoot, you made sure to look where you were putting your feet. This acquired vigilance has twice saved me from snake bite — I felt the movement before the snake attacked. It has also served me well in my new metropolitan existence. Unlike my friends who complain endlessly about the foulness of London streets, I never step in dog mess. My African upbringing has trained me to look where I'm going.

In all my years in Africa I rarely remember being frightened of the wildlife. Animals have always been my great passion. I can remember the names of every dog I have ever played with or taken for a walk, even when I struggle to recall its owner's name. Later on, when I went away to school, I pitied the European children I met. They had to be content with mere cats and dogs as pets, while I had exotic creatures like mongooses, chimps and cheetahs as my playmates.

3

Memsahib Kidogo

Africa in the Twenties was a primitive place, especially to Europeans used to a high degree of mod cons. The people on whom the settlers relied for any degree of efficiency or comfort were the servants. We had electricity at Seremai supplied by the water-powered dynamo in the coffee factory, but it only worked after dark. If anyone wanted to listen to the radio in the daytime they had to connect it to a car battery. The dynamo was turned off when we went to bed. If there was a party, as there often was, one of the houseboys had to stay at his post in the pantry — asleep on the floor, usually, rolled up in a blanket — until the last guest had gone. Then began a curious ritual reminiscent of a Charlie Chaplin film. JC would kick the boy awake with the bellowed command, '*Setima!*' This is the Swahili word for 'steam' but was widely used to translate 'electricity'. The boy had then to run down the hairpin bend track to the coffee factory at the foot of the hill and rouse the boy sleeping next to the dynamo with the same bellowed '*Setima!*' so that he would switch it off. After that it was hurricane lamps and candles.

In those days the efforts of the servants were taken for granted by their white masters, most of who regarded the Africans as subhuman. The

43

cooks, in particular, had a hard time of it. It was their job to prepare and elaborate unfamiliar European food on the unwieldy wood-burning Dover stoves favoured by the settlers, which had no heat settings. On top of that, when there was a party they were expected to be flexible and uncomplaining — serving a perfect lunch five hours later than it was originally ordered because the guests had preferred to carry on drinking — and to cater for anything up to a dozen unscheduled guests. With drinks, 'first toasties' would be served. This is a colonial tradition of serving hot savouries — such as anchovies on toast — with pre-dinner drinks. (The Africans couldn't pronounce it and called it 'firsty toasties'.) In many heavy-drinking European households, dinner had often not been called for several hours after first toasties had been and gone. The boys were rarely praised, frequently shouted at and sometimes hit.

There was something singularly unfair about the way the Europeans bemoaned the Africans' lack of civilisation and polish, while withholding from them the conditions in which such attributes flourish. Unlike them, we had running water for our bathrooms and lavatories, and hot water at that. The daily bath was taken as normal by colonials — personal hygiene was essential in the heat — and hygiene standards back in Europe often shocked us. John Carberry was so appalled at the twice-weekly bath that was considered adequate at one of my Swiss finishing schools that he wrote to the headmistress stipulating that I bath every day. (Due to a

44

Victorian interpretation of medicine, which stood common sense on its head, when we had the curse we were not permitted to bath at all.)

The plumbing at Seremai was a marvel of simple science. Water which supplied the whole estate — two houses, the coffee farm, the stables, gardens etc. — was pumped up from the Chania river to a steel-plated tank measuring about twenty feet square by ten feet high. This was known as a Braithwaite tank and was the type used by the railway to provide steam for their locomotives. The tank was mounted on thirty-foot high metal stilts, which looked like a giant version of my Meccano set. Hot water for the bathrooms came from another 'tank', which in reality was a forty-four-gallon oil drum, laid on its side. This was sited much nearer the ground on a system of stone supports, rather like a home-made barbecue and under this, in the early morning and again in the evening, a wood fire was lit. If you wanted a bath in the afternoon you would tell the kitchen *toto* to light the fire. Because of the red earth the water came out of the tap brown. One of the pleasures of bathing was to lie quite still in the bath and watch my belly-button fill up with mud. The water needed to be filtered for drinking by a gadget which stood in the pantry, looked as if it hailed from the early days of the Industrial Revolution and had to have things called candle filters bought for it.

The houseboys' living conditions, in contrast, were spartan in the extreme. At Seremai, as in all other colonial households, their quarters were sited away from the house. They were tin-roofed stone huts resembling bleak monastic cells and were discreetly screened off by a row of gum trees. The boys' quarters were strictly out of bounds to me. Europeans complained that the Africans stank; however, as it was extremely cold at night and in the early morning at Nyeri, and they had only cold water to wash in and pit latrines, that did not seem too surprising.

In contrast to the adults who, as I have said, regarded Africans as subhuman, I formed strong bonds of friendship with many of our houseboys. Fraternising with the Africans was frowned on by the adults at Seremai but I was happily unaware of the barriers of race or caste. I regarded the *totos* as my playmates. In years to come, as my relationship with those who were supposed to care for me deteriorated, some of the older houseboys displayed a protectiveness towards me which came close to conspiracy. When I was locked in my room they used to smuggle food in to me, a crime for which they risked being sacked. I learned their language through talking to them as equals and was soon fluent in Swahili, which is the great umbrella language of East Africa. I even learned some Kikuyu, which gave me an advantage over most adults who struggled, as the English invariably do with foreign languages, to communicate with the Africans. This was partly due to arrogance as most Europeans regarded it as beneath them to master the language of the natives. With few exceptions (the Trenches being one), the settlers communicated with the Africans via a strangled

46

version of Swahili known as 'ki-settler'. Looking back, I regard it as an absolute miracle that the Africans ever understood what the women who ran these colonial households were telling them to do. Despite having lived in Kenya for most of his adult life, John Carberry never mastered more than a few words. '*Setima*' was one. '*Sukuma*' was another, often qualified by '*pole pole*' or its opposite '*pesi pesi*'. These were used when the boys were putting his aircraft away in the hangar. '*Sukuma*' means 'push'; '*pole pole*' means 'slowly or carefully', while '*pesi pesi*' means 'hurry up, get on with it'. The expression used most frequently by whites when talking to African labour on the coffee farm at Seremai — Africans are noisy workers — was '*watcha kelele*': 'shut up'.

All the servants at Seremai were male, as was the case throughout colonial Africa, except where female ayahs were employed. Ours were all from the Kikuyu tribe because our estate was on Kikuyu land. In those days all Africans had tribal markings, a hangover from the days of constant tribal wars. The marks were a means of identifying your own dead after a battle. Kikuyus used to pierce the ears of their children and stretch the hole with larger and larger wooden discs so that often the lobes of adults hung down to their shoulders. These hanging lobes were called *ndebes*. When Kikuyus joined the police they were required to tidy up these lobes, which they did by hanging them over the tops of their ears. The other feature that characterised Kikuyus was a gap between their lower teeth in

47

the middle. This was the result of removing both front teeth in childhood as a protection against tetanus, which was rife in Africa in those days. If lockjaw set in, food could still be taken through the gap.

Status-conscious settlers from the notorious Happy Valley set had Somali servants. They were regarded as more up-market, more on a par with the English butler than your everyday Kikuyu houseboys. We had a permanent house staff of six who led a virtually celibate life as their womenfolk lived separately from them on the reserve, which began beyond the boundary of our land. Their function was looking after the children and growing food. Women appeared at Seremai only during the coffee harvest when they worked as pickers. The houseboys got to see their wives when they went on leave, which was once a year and sometimes not as often as that.

The servants wore long cotton robes called *kanzus* and red fezes on their heads. The everyday *kanzu* was a rusty brown. But when our head houseboy, Gatimu, waited at table he changed his brown kanzu for a white one with a sleeveless red bolero trimmed with gold braid over it. Under their *kanzus* they wore shorts. I knew this because all Kikuyus take snuff, which they call *bakki*. Kamau, who looked after me, kept his snuff in a tin in his shorts pocket. Every now and then he would hoik up his *kanzu*, produce the tin from his shorts pocket and noisily snort a pinch of snuff up each nostril.

We never knew how old the Africans were because the Kikuyu counted their age not from

48

birth but from the date of their circumcision and they were circumcised in groups, which could comprise an age range of five years or more. I never saw a circumcision but we always knew when one was happening from the noise the women made. The ceremony used to take place early in the morning down by the river. The boys, who were between eleven and sixteen, would be made to stand in the river, the idea being that the freezing water would numb their parts. It was considered unmanly to show pain and so, to drown out their screams, the women would make that strange high-pitched noise · called ululation, which is so characteristic of African tribeswomen. The girls were circumcised too, but even when I was a child I found it difficult to make any contact with African women not only because they stayed on the reserve but because they didn't speak Swahili, only Kikuyu, which made communication difficult. When I tried to speak to them they would explode in shrieks of self-conscious mirth, so I soon gave up. Besides, they stank, not of body odour but of the skins they wore instead of woven cloth. These were oiled with castor oil, a plant that grew in abundance up-country. But beauty is in the eye of the beholder: Waiganjo, who looked after JC's planes, told me that whenever he went home his mother said *he* stank — of soap!

At Seremai we were unusual because we always had a European housekeeper, a legacy, perhaps, of JC's aristocratic background. The housekeeper's function was to order and keep an eye on stores of food and drink, the assumption being that a European was likely to be more trustworthy than an African. Alas, this was not to be the case. One was found to have drunk all the booze in the store. Her peccadillo was not discovered until after she had left because she had thoughtfully refilled the whisky bottles with tea and the gin bottles with water.

Among the African staff, Gatimu regarded himself as a cut above the other boys because he could speak some English, shoot a gun and drive a car. He looked after the master bedroom and waited at table. He often doubled as a driver; Waiganjo looked after the aeroplane; Kamau looked after me; Mathenge was the pantry boy, Kimani was the cook, while another boy, known as the kitchen *toto*, washed up the pots and pans. The only servant who wasn't Kikuyu was Anderea, the *dhobi*, or laundry boy, who was a Ugandan. His job was hard as all the washing was done by hand in cold water. He had a big, heavy iron, which was heated by burning charcoal. The *dhobi* would spend all his time blowing the charcoal to get it hot and then, when it was, little sparks would blow out and unfailingly burn holes in the clothes.

Anderea, the *dhobi*, also played a second role. The word '*fundi*' means 'expert' or 'fixer'. When it came to jiggers Anderea was the *fundi* you needed. They are one of the hazards of living in Africa. The jigger is an insect, a bit like a flea, the female of which likes to lay her eggs in a hole she has made in your skin, usually in the corner of the nail on your big toe. The adults used to

50

louse their shoes with paraffin to deter them, but as I always went barefoot I was forever getting them. When you have jiggers in your toe they itch like holy hell. You tend to discover you've got one lying in bed at night and you find yourself rubbing your toe up and down on the sheet to get rid of the itch. To get them out, Anderea used the point of a safety pin, which he burned black in a candle flame. Then he would delicately peel the skin of the toe back and lift out the bag of eggs without breaking it. You had to wait until the moment was right and often, if I went to Anderea as soon as I had got the jigger, he would send me away and tell me to come back the next day. The thing was that if you tried to get the jigger out too soon you might break the egg sack. Then the result was an infected toe. When the bag, which was about the size of a small pea, came out in one piece you could see the jigger in the middle, like a black dot. At that moment Anderea would shout triumphantly, Angalia!' — 'Look!' — hold it in the candle flame and burn the lot. Once Dickie, the eldest son of my first governess, got a jigger in the end of his penis — all little kids used to run around naked and roll in the dust in Africa. Having it removed — by the classic Anderea method — must have been excruciating. I recall much yelling and screaming.

As with all children of colonials, I was pampered in the sense that I always had someone to wait on me and perform the onerous chores. Like most other European children, from my birth — while my parents were jet-setting around the world and I was running barefoot and half naked in Africa, hardly aware I had parents — my care was the responsibility of a selection of hired hands, some white, some African. For the first seven years of my life I had a mother substitute in the shape of Kathleen Carlysle, an English-trained nanny, whom my mother had hired through the *Tatler*. My abiding memory of Kathleen, or Girlie as I called her, was that she wore a gold slave bangle and that she adored me. She later married the manager of the Standard Bank in Nyeri, our nearest town, where I used to visit her and her two Kerry Blue dogs, Kerry and Rebel.

My other carer was Kamau, my African ayah. Kamau was elderly and kind, with a strange circular dent in the middle of his forehead. He addressed me either as *memsahib kidogo* (little mistress) or *m'toto* (*toto* is Swahili for child). His job was to look after my personal needs. If I wanted a bath Kamau ran it — and cleaned the bath afterwards. He made my bed, tidied my room and picked up the clothes I stepped out of at night and took them to the *dhobi*, whence they would emerge clean and pressed. Kamau also served my food, but it was the European Girlie who ate with me and taught me my table manners.

Our day began early. Girlie would get me up and help me dress, and then we would breakfast together. In those days children didn't eat with grown-ups. I ate my meals in a room we called the sun parlour, but which functioned as a day nursery. Colonials rarely ate African food,

Breakfast would start with porridge, followed by eggs and bacon, sometimes sausages, kidneys and black pudding, or scrambled eggs. Girlie was kind but she was strict, too. I would be expected to eat up all my porridge. If I didn't, back it would come, grey and congealed, at lunch-time.

I was a small, skinny child who, it was felt, needed building up. So every day after breakfast I was given a spoonful of Kepplers malt. For the rest of the morning I'd be expected to amuse myself and was left largely unsupervised. There was so much to do I was never bored. I pedalled my tricycle up and down the veranda and wheeled Flopsy, my cat, around in my doll's pram — I never liked dolls and always preferred to play with live toys. This led to tragedy on one occasion when I left Flopsy in the doll's pram with my pet rabbit and returned to find the cat had eaten the rabbit.

From a very early age I loved horses. I had a traditional rocking-horse in the sun parlour, which I rode vigorously, but I graduated to the real thing while I was still a baby. My mother had had a very old white Somali pony called Mafuta, which means 'fat' in Swahili. With Mafuta came a curious object which had probably been made for her when she was a baby — a cross between a saddle and a chair, made of wicker. This curious contraption would be strapped on to Mafuta and I would be lifted on to it and solemnly led round the farm by the syce (groom) who was called Njeroge.

As I grew older I was able to ride on my own. I took for granted the wide open spaces where I

53

could wander with my pony for hours withou
the inconvenience of gates or fences to worr
about. I loved the rich variety of the wildlife in
my part of Africa. I treasured the fact that exotic
animals like elephants and leopards shared the
Highlands with me and that if we drove to the
plains at Nanyuki, thirty-odd miles away, I would
see giraffes, gazelles (which we called buck) of all
kinds — impala, Thomson's, Granty — and the
very rare Grevy's zebra that was only found
up-country, and which in my view was much
more beautiful than the common Burchell's
variety found all over Kenya. We even had our
own rare type of giraffe, known as the
Reticulated giraffe, which is a beautiful animal
with almost chestnut-brown patches separated
by finer white lines.

I would also play with the dogs and was a keen
gardener, having watched the *shamba* boys
(gardeners) working in our large vegetable patch
I had my own small piece of garden quite close
to the house where I grew radishes, which were
rewarding because they germinated so fast, and
carrots, which required a bit more patience.

Lunch was served in the sun parlour for me
and Kathleen at one o'clock and was, again, a
very English meal, beginning with soup — as did
dinner — followed by plain roast meat with
boiled potatoes and other vegetables, or fried
tilapia fish from the river. Again I was expected
to leave nothing on my plate. If I took two
potatoes I would be expected to eat two
Pudding might be rice pudding which I loved
jelly, or junket which I hated because I was

convinced it was sour milk. 'Come along. Eat up,' Girlie would coax. 'Think of the starving in China.'

After lunch, much against my will, I would be put to bed for my rest. I always loathed the afternoon lie-down. Of course, it was just a method of getting me out of the way so that the adults could take a nap, but I always thought it so unfair. They stayed up late, drinking and partying, and may have needed a midday rest. I didn't and just lay on my bed feeling bored.

When I got up we had English-style afternoon tea — bread and butter, sandwiches and cakes, none of which I liked. In the afternoons I would roam about, happily exploring by myself. People imagine only children are lonely and Seremai was extremely isolated, but I was very self-sufficient. I didn't particularly like other children. I enjoyed doing things that were regarded as odd. Once I found a dead lizard and decided to dissect it. I knew about innards from visits to the butcher's and I was most concerned that I couldn't find any kidneys in the lizard. I rushed about asking Girlie and the Africans, and any adults I could find, how lizards managed without kidneys but no one seemed to know.

From the toys I played with it is clear that if John Carberry had wanted an heir at all it was a son and not a daughter. What I grew up with were a Hornby train set, which was always out on the floor, and a Meccano kit. JC's prejudice also dictated my appearance. Girls in this era usually wore pretty smocked dresses and had long hair, lovingly curled, but I was invariably dressed in shorts and obliged to wear my hair short. The dreadful bob — straight-across fringe with, horror of horrors, *the tips of the ear lobes showing* — was cut every few weeks by Maxwell Trench, who also cut Nellie's hair. Although I longed to have long hair I was delighted not to have to wear dresses. Dressing up is something I have always hated. There were times, however, even at Seremai when, much to my disgust, I was made to put on a dress and expected to behave like a young lady. From about the age of five I would be invited to children's parties, which were usually held at the Nyeri Club. The farms up-country were often miles from each other and this was a way European children could get together and ostensibly make friends. I wasn't fond of other children and I detested these gatherings. I would be expected to put on shoes and socks. Girlie would do things to my hair and force me into a party dress made of stiff organza which scratched under the arms. Everything on these occasions was done to replicate children's parties back 'home'. There were all sorts of goodies to eat — jelly set into orange skins, iced biscuits in the shape of animals, chocolate cake and meringues, which I loved — and boring bread and butter. Nellie took me to one and insisted I eat some bread and butter first. But I wanted to leave room for the meringues and jellies, so I began to whinge. Whenever I was picky about my food, Nellie Trench would remind me of the time I sat at the Nyeri Club in front of a plateful of untouched bread and butter, bellowing 'but I'm *starving*'.

My colonial childhood means that to this day I loathe cooking or anything to do with food preparation. I was a privileged child never to be made to clear any of the mess I created and to be surrounded by such warm and caring servants.

4

A Tough Breed

As JC was not interested in me, in the years that followed my mother's death I spent a great deal of time at my grandmother's house in Nairobi. What did Granny think when she discovered that her only daughter's child wasn't being taught to read or write, hated wearing shoes and spoke Swahili like a native *toto*? What did she think of her son-in-law?

I can only guess at Granny's feelings from her reactions to me. I was expected to put on a dress when I stayed with her and to wear socks and shoes. One day when I was about six I was sitting with her on the veranda. I had my shoes up under me on the chair and Granny told me to sit properly as it wasn't ladylike to show your knickers. I was also expected to do lessons. Granny had five children, four of whom were sons. The eldest was Uncle Gerald, a surgeon in Nairobi, who lived not far from his mother and also had five children. I was particularly friendly with two of the girls, Patty and Robin. They always wore dresses and had lovely long hair, which I envied desperately. When I stayed with Granny a Frenchwoman called Mam'selle came in to teach me and my cousins our lessons. She awarded us pink, blue and yellow cards at the end of the day to indicate effort and progress.

58

Pink was good, blue was middling and yellow was 'could do better'. In the evening we had to take them in to the drawing-room to show them to Granny. I was not interested in formalised learning and found lessons boring. Patty's card was always pink and mine was always yellow.

Life at Riverside Lodge, where Granny presided with her second husband Rudolph Mayer, was quaintly old-fashioned and formal. In those days they still had rickshaws in the city and I can remember being pulled through the streets by an African in one of these two-wheeled carts as we went to lay flowers on my mother's grave. Although the house had a long drive, and grounds large enough for stables and servants' quarters (and chickens), you could see other houses all round.

One luxury Granny possessed that we didn't have at Seremai, being very isolated, was a telephone. It didn't have a dial and the mouthpiece was screwed on to the wall. To get the operator you wound a handle and told him the number you wanted. The Africans loved the coming of the telephone because it gave them access to copper wire, which they made into earrings. For this reason the telephones rarely worked.

When I think of Granny I see an ample woman, dressed in old-fashioned colourless clothes, with a mass of fluffy hair. Rudolph was a portly moustachioed man with a thick foreign accent, which I now realise was German. None of the cousins called him 'Grandad', instead we addressed him as 'Uncle'. Granny was kind and solicitous but displayed that rather rigid approach to child-rearing that characterised the Victorians. She gave us syrup of figs every day to ensure that we were 'regular'. If she suspected this was not the case, she upped the dose to the more draconian liquid paraffin. She also believed that if children ate too much at night they got nightmares, so instead of the cooked meal I was used to taking with Girlie, at Granny's I got only a glass of milk and some bread and butter, strewn incongruously with rainbow-coloured hundreds and thousands, and went to bed starving. To make it worse the milk was boiled: Granny was being hygiene-conscious, of course, for milk in Africa came from an unwashed teat pulled by an unwashed hand, but I didn't mind. I have always loathed boiled milk.

As at Seremai, I didn't eat with the grown-ups. I ate my 'supper' with Mam'selle and then was expected to go into the drawing-room and say good night. The adults would be having drinks and first toasties. I was not used to kissing and disliked having to do it. Often some of our uncles would be there. One of them, Rudolph, Granny's second youngest child, seemed to dislike this ritual as much as I did. I hated kissing him most of all. He had a very bristly face and it was like kissing a cactus.

Granny tried hard to civilise me — with limited success. Once, while I was staying with her, one of her dogs had puppies. I have always had rather unpredictable tastes and Granny caught me eating puppy food. She was horrified and told me it was made from puppy-dog tails.

60

As most dogs in Africa had their tails docked I thought it might be true and it put me off for a while. But the habit returned later. When I got my own pony I shared its meals of bran and barley. As for dog biscuits, I found them nice and crunchy.

When I used to visit her at Riverside Lodge, Granny was ultra-respectable — a venerable and financially successful pillar of the colony's business establishment. She and Rudolph had built up the largest newspaper empire in East Africa, as well as owning the freehold on many of Nairobi's most prestigious office buildings. But I discovered later that Granny's youth had been far from conventional, that she been involved in a passionate *ménage à trois* for some years and that the reasons I called her second husband 'Uncle' were devious indeed.

Granny called her fifth and last child, who was my mother, Maïa Anderson because her husband's name was Anderson. But it was an open secret in Nairobi that Maïa and her older brother, my bristly Uncle Rudolph, were the children, not of my grandmother's husband Alfred Anderson, but his business colleague and close friend Rudolph Mayer. About the time my mother went off to school in Belgium, Granny (who was also called Maïa) had divorced Anderson and married Mayer. But Uncle Rudolph and my mother were born while she was still married to Anderson. Genes have blown a hole in many an elaborately constructed alibi. In accordance with the social codes of the day, Rudolph Mayer was invariably referred to as my mother's stepfather, but as the years went by her brother Rudolph grew into a clone of Mayer, so much so that people seeing him seated at his desk at the *East African Standard*, long after Mayer's death, thought they were looking at a ghost.

Granny was born Emma Louise Antoinette Troissaert of a good family in Ghent in 1874. Some time around 1890 she went to England, probably to learn English, and met Alfred Anderson, who was a vicar's son from Wiltshire. They were married, without Maïa's father's blessing, in September 1891. Alfred's family seem to have been equally unenthusiastic about the union, for the wedding present to the young couple from Alfred's father was £50 and a one-way ticket to South Africa. Granny and Alfred remained in South Africa throughout the years of the Boer War and had three sons, Gerald, Claud and Charles. They were extremely poor during these years. Gerald's early childhood memories are of home being a humble hut lit by a paraffin lamp with maize porridge the staple dish.

Rudolph Mayer was a Bavarian Jew who had decided to seek his fortune in South Africa. He had a camera and began his professional life photographing farmers in the veld. As Alfred was a newspaperman all his life it is possible that journalism introduced them. Family tradition has it that Mayer fell in love with my grandmother from the start and, though this may have been part of a myth-building stratagem designed to legitimise their adultery, it is not hard to see why. Youthful photographs show Granny as a confident woman possessed of a certain lush beauty, ample of build, with a direct gaze and sensual-looking features. Whatever the tortured private feelings of each member of this unconventional trio were, for years they were inseparable — and interdependent.

It was my grandmother who decreed that they should leave war-torn South Africa, where they were ceaselessly hard up, and try life in a gentler part of the colonial world. Her new base was eventually to deliver all the things so far denied her — respectability, power, wealth.

In 1900 there were very few white people in Mombasa and the first thing Granny did was to set up a laundry catering for them. Her next venture was to buy a run-down establishment optimistically named the Grand Hotel. This was less successful than the laundry, mainly because of the tradition of the waiters to give customers chits instead of taking money. Normally it worked reasonably well, as customers usually paid up in the end. On one fateful occasion, however, the waiters gave chits to an unusually copious clientele who came, unbeknown to them, from a large passenger ship. The customers left port the next day before settling their bills and the Grand Hotel foundered.

While my grandmother busied herself with a succession of business enterprises her private life became increasingly tangled. In 1901, soon after her arrival in Mombasa, she gave birth to her fourth son, Rudolph, who was Mayer's child. Three years later she had my mother, also his.

Who can say, from such a distance, what were the rights and wrongs of this case? While I was growing up the family's sympathies seemed to lie with Mayer. We were told that Alfred had been a taciturn, morose-seeming man with a twilight private life of his own. Gerald remembers riding pillion on his father's motorbike on regular trips up-country to Thika, ostensibly to search for timber, and having to wait for him in hotels while he consorted with dusky Somali women.

Despite the emotional tangle the two men continued to work together. Their business took off when they bought an Indian hand press and used it to bring out, on coloured paper — which was all they could get — the first edition of the *Mombasa Times*. Later on they moved up to Nairobi and started the *East African Standard*, with Mayer representing the business end of the operation as MD, and Anderson the news-gathering side. This was the start of the hugely lucrative East African newspaper monopoly that came to include the *Ugandan Argus* and the *Tanganyika Standard*.

In 1912 Granny divorced Alfred, suffering excommunication from the Roman Catholic Church in the process. Four years later in the church of St Stephen in Nairobi she married Mayer. Bowing to the inevitable, Alfred did the decent thing. He gallantly surrendered the field to his one-time friend and rival, and left the continent.

As a child I was unaware that there was anything unusal about either my grandmother's home or my father's. Although, unlike at home, I

64

was never afraid of being beaten at my grandmother's house in Nairobi, I was neverthe-less always glad to go back to the freedom of up-country life after a stint at Granny's. And at Seremai, while I found no affection from my father, I was able to witness and benefit from the warm family environment at the home of Maxwell Trench.

The Carberry–Trench partnership was an odd affair as the two men could not have been more different. JC was an Irish aristocrat who had come to Africa essentially to escape his mother and rewrite his personal history. He exploited the continent's natural resources in order to pursue the white man's hobbies — big-game hunting, deep-sea fishing, etc. He relished Kenya's cloudless skies because they made light work of flying his planes, but he never really got under the skin of Africa and remained a man most at ease in big cities. Temperamentally he was a schemer, a nurser of grudges and, I suspect, a coward.

Maxwell was impulsive, fiery and not averse to using his fists to settle scores. Many years later he and JC fell out over the business. Maxwell believed, probably with justification, that JC had swindled him and beat him up outside the Palace Hotel in Mombasa. JC was terrified and took to carrying knuckledusters when he went out in case he ran into Maxwell.

Maxwell was a distinctive figure, his tall, sinewy frame invariably clad in its uniform of well-worn sun-bleached shorts, topped with the old army beret he had acquired at the outbreak of the Great War still sporting its brass East Africa Regiment badge. He had made Kenya his home after discovering that the British Colonial Office was looking for a Coffee Adviser for British East Africa. After starting off in Nairobi he'd moved to Nyeri, where he'd built a house just a few hundred yards from my family home at Seremai. By the time I was born he had already been in partnership with Carberry for nearly ten years.

Maxwell, who, unlike John Carberry, had spent all his life in the tropics, adapted to life in Kenya as if he had been born there. Having worked continuously with coloured people he knew that the way to get the best out of them was to talk to them in their language and so, unlike most of the British settlers, his Swahili was fluent. He loved nature and possessed a profound and detailed knowledge of the flora and fauna of East Africa, a passion he bequeathed to me. It was he who taught me — solemnly testing me to see if I had retained them — the names and properties of all the plants, and the defining features and dispositions of the creatures.

Maxwell was married to Nellie, a warm-hearted woman with a rather dumpy figure, wispy hair and light-blue smiling eyes. They had three children — Jack and Nancy, who were almost grown-up when I was a child, and Dan, who was five years older than me. The Trenches' was an extremely loving marriage. Nellie was a generous and tolerant woman who had insisted that Maxwell acknowledge and support an llegitimate daughter he had sired years earlier with a house servant in Jamaica. Theirs was a noisy, volatile, loving household, which I treated like a second home in the years before my first boarding-school took me across away from Seremai.

In contrast to the Carberry household, where the adults partied late and rarely rose before noon, the Trenches' house was a busy place. Nellie always rose before daybreak to supervise the labour arriving to work on the coffee plantation and to work in the dairy, which supplied the estate with milk, cream and butter. Children get up early so in the years before I went to school I used to go round to the Trenches to help at the dairy. Nellie had a herd of humpback Zebu cattle. They were milked twice a day the way they are in England, but there was no cowshed. The cow would be caught where she stood, her hocks would be tied together with a strip of leather called a *riem* to stop her kicking and she would be milked there and then, the milker not sitting on a stool, but squatting. If she had a calf it would be held close enough for her to lick and groom it, which would encourage her to let down her milk. I loved milking, provided the cow was calm and friendly, which wasn't always the case with native cattle, where the cows were fiercer than the bulls. There was one called Murungu who was so placid I could milk her straight into my mouth. I adored that, though my aim was not always perfect and I often got the milk in my eye or down my front. I also enjoyed working the Alfa-Lavel separator

67

which divided the cream from the skimmed milk. It was quite a complicated device, with lots of discs which fitted together, but whereas never enjoyed formalised learning I took readily to anything mechanical and from quite an early age took pride in my ability to assemble this gadget.

My favourite among the Trenches' African staff was Wamaisa, the boy who looked after the cattle. He walked like a clown, due to the fact that he was missing about three toes on each foot. He told us that he'd been sleeping in the bush one night, looking after his father's livestock, when a hyena had come up and bitten off most of his toes. The Africans weren't self-conscious about blemishes or deformities. Wamaisa didn't have a hang-up about his gait but accepted it. It gave him an identity. It was those early mornings spent at the dairy that gave me my lifelong passion for skimmed milk. When they were making cream in the separator I would hold a tin under it to catch the milk as it trickled out, all bluey-white and frothy. At our house, because I was deemed skinny and in need of building up, my breakfast porridge was cloyingly doused with cream.

The Trenches' house possessed some odd features. Their bathroom had five doors, which meant that everyone was pretty relaxed about nudity as, when you walked in, there always seemed to be someone in the bath. For some reason their lavatory was outside, though reached from the bathroom, through one of the five doors. A trip to the loo was referred to as 'visiting Mr Hunter'.

Both Maxwell and Nellie had retained many of their West Indian ways. Maxwell spoke with a West Indian accent. 'Walk good,' he would say to people as they left, in a Caribbean version of 'mind how you go'. Even their cooking was West Indian. If Maxwell was eating a fried breakfast, there would always be a plantain to keep the egg and bacon company. Whereas in the Carberry household the cooking was as blandly English as the staff could manage and the staple was the ubiquitous potato, at the Trenches they ate rice with tropical vegetables like yams and cassava. It was there that I developed a taste for porcupine. These animals used to get into the vegetable garden and were trapped in sacks. They couldn't escape backwards as their quills stuck in the netting. We ate them roasted: they are delicious, with a flavour similar to pork.

I always felt loved and welcome at the Trenches' — far more so than in my own home. Nellie Trench told me many years later, after I had experienced much unhappiness and she had had to stand by helplessly, that she and Maxwell had wanted to adopt me when my mother was killed. It was John Carberry's unexpected next move that dissuaded them.

5

Junie Baby

I had just celebrated my fifth birthday when I acquired a stepmother. Of course, I wasn't involved. JC met, courted and married his third wife in England on a trip that took him away from Seremai for months.

When I think of him it is his piercing blue eyes that I see. When I remember June Carberry it is her smell that comes to me. She wore a lot of make-up and in the sunny climate of the Highlands her body gave off an odour of old-fashioned face-cream and perfume mixed with sweat. This was at its most concentrated in the closets in which she hung her vast and ever-increasing wardrobe. Its cloying memory is the reason why I never hang my clothes in a wardrobe without first having hung them up to air.

Nobody at Seremai knew that John Carberry was planning to marry again. When he appeared with his new bride, a peroxide blonde with a memorable, husky, 'gin' voice and a bold, teasing manner with men, everyone wanted to know where he had found her. Some were more surprised than others. Maxwell Trench remembered Carberry producing a blonde, whom he introduced to everyone as 'my cousin Junie'. The next time he met her it was as Mrs John Carberry.

70

Judging by her looks, manner and shadowy family background, June was clearly no lady. Some said JC had met her in South Africa. I was told, when I was a little older, that she had been a tart in Piccadilly. The truth is both more prosaic and more entertaining. An 'exclusive' article in the *Daily Mail* of 18 July 1930 headlined 'Airman Peer's Secret Wedding' quoted June, whose maiden name was Weir Mosley, as saying that the couple had met in Nairobi. According to the newspaper the wedding had taken place at St Pancras Register Office ten days earlier in circumstances of such secrecy that the bride's mother did not know until the *Daily Mail* reporter broke the news to her on her doorstep. The dialogue between the reporter and Mrs Mosley was reproduced in full in the paper.

The journalist wrote:

I called yesterday at the bride's home. When I asked for Mrs Carberry, I was informed that there was no one of that name, but Mrs Mosley, the mother, asked me to explain.

I replied that I referred to the former Miss June Weir Mosley. Mrs Mosley was astonished.

'June dear,' she called. 'Will you come downstairs a moment?'

A pretty girl, radiant in a blue dress, arrived.

'Is it true, June, that you have married Mr Carberry?' asked Mrs Mosley quietly.

'Yes, Mother, it's quite true,' was the reply, 'though I do not know how it has become

71

known. We wanted to keep it a secret till the end of the month.'

Mrs Mosley stood still for a moment smiling. Then she said to me: 'Well I am surprised. You know, I think that modern girls ought to be spanked. Fancy not telling her mother.'

It would have been hard to find a person less suited to being the stepmother of a five-year-old than June Carberry. The fact that she disliked children and did not want any herself was doubtless one of the reasons John Carberry selected her. He had, after all, tried to scupper the pregnancies of both his previous wives.

Since the days when she was simply my stepmother June Carberry has become quite well known. This is largely due to the prominent part she played in the Erroll murder trial and the interest in that period kindled by James Fox's book *White Mischief*. June Carberry's name is now synonymous with all that is most lurid about Kenya's frivolous Happy Valley set (by the time my story begins Happy Valley was not so much a place as a mindset). The goings-on of this small group of bored, decadent, up-country settlers has captured the public imagination. I deplore the fact that to some people the behaviour of a small crowd of shallow social butterflies has become synonymous with Kenya settlers in general. The vast majority of these were upright, decent people who, in the absence of inherited fortunes, had their living to earn. It was my misfortune that I grew up in a household which subscribed to the values of the fast crowd.

The people for whom the expression 'Happy Valley' was coined lived near the Wanjohe river in the Aberdares. I have often wondered since whether the customs of the residents gave the river its name. In Kikuyu '*njohe*' means 'booze' — it was what they called their local brew, made from sugar cane or fermented maize — while '*wa*' means 'people of'.

June Carberry came with natural qualifications for membership of the Happy Valley set. True, she had no social pedigree but they were a democratic lot, provided you were fun and uninhibited. June was a heavy drinker, becoming louder and more animated as the night wore on; she also used drugs, or dope as she and her friends used to call it. She kept a syringe in her bathroom at Seremai, an old-fashioned-looking thing such as a vet might use today, made of glass with a white metal plunger. Her main interest, however, was sex. She picked up men on boats, in bars, by swimming pools, in hotels . . . But what really made her eligible was boredom. Unlike Nellie Trench, who was a skilful manager and up at cock-crow each day, June had no taste for hard labour. Married to John Carberry, she didn't need to work. She never succeeded in creating a role for herself at Seremai. I can remember doing lots of things with Nellie Trench, but my memories of June usually involve journeys out of Africa. She didn't ride, she didn't play tennis, she didn't shoot and she never learned to fly. She fiddled around at several business ventures but none of them came to anything. At one stage she imported some nutria, a creature like a coypu which is a native of South America, with the intention of farming them for their fur. But the nutria escaped and, not being native, caused a great deal of damage to fish stocks in the river. Later there was an attempt to breed Siamese cats. But June was impractical and lacked staying power, so her business schemes came to nothing.

June Carberry was an uncomplicated good-time girl and took to the hedonistic colonial life like a duck to water. Like many children of my generation I kept an autograph book with which I pestered passing adults. In addition to signing their names, subjects were required to answer certain questions. June Carberry's list of her favourite animal/pastime/book/film/career provides a telling glimpse of her tastes and values. To 'what is your favourite pastime' she has answered 'dancing'. To 'what is your best subject', 'My Self' [sic]. To 'what is your favourite sport', 'haven't got one'. To 'what do you want to do when you leave school?', 'go round the world' and to 'what is your favourite book?', *Gone with the Wind*'.

She was pretty, though not elegant, and had a good body which she liked to show off. It was not only I who was used to seeing her walking about naked. Ralfe Hutchinson, whose parents were friends of John Carberry's, and who was five years younger than me, remembers June enjoying wandering around her bedroom naked 'even if us young boys were there'.

Unlike the pioneer settlers who feared Africa's

fierce sun and always wore hats, June came from the generation which discovered sunbathing and made suntans fashionable. Up-country where it wasn't so hot she usually wore slacks. At the coast she would display her suntanned legs in the shortest of shorts. Clothes were her passion. She used to go to Europe on fashion shopping sprees and was generous with her old clothes, regularly making space for new purchases by giving garments she was tired of to friends.

Despite the fact that Seremai was very isolated, June, taking the view that you never knew who might turn up, was always elaborately made up with carefully applied bright-red lipstick and matching nails. Her favourite brands were Max Factor and Cyclax. As a child I used to like to sit in her bedroom and watch her put on her make-up — she would often give me some — and when I was older she would pay me pocket money for plucking her eyebrows and giving her manicures. Her taste for bright colours soon made itself felt in the house. This was the early Thirties and, keen to be in the swim of art deco interior design, June had the doors and mantelpiece painted in black gloss, while the walls were done in a vivid shade of raspberries and cream.

I saw June Carberry through the eyes of a child and — irony of ironies — a child who wanted a mother. In fact, though she wasn't always very nice to me, I think I loved her. But it was one-sided. The discovery that a marriage she saw as socially desirable brought with it baggage in the shape of what she invariably referred to as 'the brat' must have been an unwelcome one. But in JC's world nothing was ever for nothing and in marrying June he was looking for someone to dump me on. June was no more physically affectionate towards me than JC and I never remember a kiss or a hug from her. She vastly preferred animals. Her favourite was a dachshund called Minnie. In my hunger for affection I became increasingly jealous of Minnie. The frustration built up over quite a while as June made it clear time and time again that Minnie meant far more to her than I did. I would come rushing in from outside, the way kids do, full of something I wanted to share with her. She would be playing with the dog. Instead of turning her attention to me she'd say, 'Don't interrupt, Juanita. Can't you see I'm talking to Minnie?' Once I was eating a big cooked breakfast. I loved kidneys and was saving it till last because it was my favourite. June knew I loved them — and what I was doing. She decided to teach me a lesson. Perhaps it wasn't good manners to keep the best till last. At any rate she said to Minnie: 'Look, Juanita doesn't like kidney.' Then she picked it off my plate and fed it to the dog. I was livid. I found Minnie later and kicked and shouted at her. Immediately I had done it I was overwhelmed with remorse and tried to cuddle her and say sorry, but she was frightened and would have none of it, cowering and snarling at me. I used to cry about it for ages afterwards, asking myself how I could have done such a horrible thing.

June spent a lot of time in bed, either lazing or

entertaining her lovers. The bed she chose was so huge the uprights of the windows had to be removed to get it in. I was afraid of the dark — and at Seremai it was very dark at night. I was not allowed to have a night-light and so, when JC was away, I would ask if I could sleep in June's bed for comfort. One night I woke up and found her hand between my legs. Embarrassed, I pushed it away thinking she must be asleep and not know what she was doing. But the hand returned. I pushed it away again. No reference was ever made to it.

When June was not in bed she was lazing in the large *en suite* bathroom, which had a magnificent sunken bath. Away from Seremai her trade mark was her car, a Ford V8, which she changed every year but which always had the same number plate: A3000.

When I was six I made my first sea voyage with June. Every year she went to England to visit her mother in London and to my delight I went with her. Often, on the way back, we would stop in the South of France for a holiday where JC would join us. He never came with us by ship, probably preferring to fly instead. In those days the journey lasted between two and three weeks and, with the number of treats and on-board entertainments provided, was like a holiday in itself. We always travelled with the same shipping company — the German East Africa line — who operated a fleet of passenger cargo ships. We embarked at Mombasa, sailing up the east coast of Africa into the Red Sea through the Gulf of Aden and up the Suez Canal. I was in my element on board these ships. Even at six I was interested in practical things and I used to make straight for the ship's carpenter and offer my services to him. Sailors love children and were happy to take me off June's hands, leaving her free to pursue her adult adventures. Those ships had small canvas swimming pools and when I was not with the carpenter I would spend hours in the pool. For the adults there were games such as shuffle board, which attracted serious betting, tenni-quoits and a strange game called horse-racing. This consisted of a strip of canvas about fifteen feet long and three feet wide, and a selection of wooden horses. When someone turned a handle a ratchet caused the horses to shudder forward. There were fancy dress parties, too, which, not being a gregarious child, I loathed.

My favourite bit of the trip was the Suez Canal. Once a ship entered, it was besieged by little boats, all rowing out furiously from the banks. These bum boats were manned by Egyptian hustlers in *kanzus* with dirty bits of cloth wound round their heads keen to sell their wares of dirty postcards, Spanish fly and, something that puzzled me as a child, 'genuine Persian carpets made in Belgium'. I was perplexed by the postcards, too. I expected the girls in the photographs to be totally naked but these were old sepia postcards shot in the Twenties and the women wore stockings rolled down to just below their knees — and shoes!

The great excitement about going through the Suez Canal were the mooring boats, which actually came aboard. In those days it was an extremely busy thoroughfare and a breakdown could mean one ship ramming another. To ensure against this every ship transported its own mooring boat while it was in the canal. If you were sailing north it would come aboard at Port Tawfiq. If you were on your way south to Mombasa the mooring boat would come aboard at Port Suez. Like the bum boats, they would row out to the ship and be lifted aboard, with the two-man crew still *in situ*, by the ship's derricks. If all went well they remained in their boat on deck until the ship was ready to leave the canal. But in the event of engine failure the boat would be launched and the crew would row like mad for the bank, carrying a mooring rope to make the ship fast to one of the many bollards that lined the banks on both sides.

Everyone was delighted when we arrived at Port Said as this was the first opportunity for us all to stretch our legs on land since the start of the voyage and the chance to visit the shops and the fleshpots. As you sailed up the canal you passed Port Said's answer to Harrods, the department store Simon Artz. June and I always stopped here to buy Turkish Delight. The other thing I looked forward to at Port Said was the gully-gully man. He was a conjurer who came on board and did a magic show on the passenger deck. To my endless mystification he could reach behind my ear and produce fluffy yellow day-old chicks.

The journey to England continued across the Mediterranean to Marseilles or Genoa, where we took the train up to Calais and then crossed the Channel. June's mother Gwynne Weir Mosley who in 1930 had told the man from the *Daily Mail* that daughters who don't confide in their mothers ought to be smacked, lived in a basement flat in Bayswater with a man called Jock to whom she was not married. Both Gwynne and Jock were very kind and I was fond of them. Gwynne had three dogs — two Pekinese and a little old creature called Cuppie she had got from London Zoo, who was half dingo. I used to take all three for walks in Hyde Park. One day on this trip I was standing watching the horses in Rotten Row when a strange, dishevelled woman came up to me and tried to persuade me to go with her. When I refused she became very aggressive and threatened to call a policeman. I told her I didn't mind because I wasn't afraid of policemen and ran away. I told June's mother what had happened and she devised an ingenious way of discouraging me from talking to strangers. She told me that people who wanted to steal children stuck needles in them to make them unconscious.

June was not the proverbial wicked stepmother and sometimes she even spoiled me with treats. On one occasion when we had come to London to visit her mother she took me to Hamleys. I was told I could choose whatever I wanted and picked a large horse made of imitation pony skin with a saddle and bridle you could remove and a flowing mane and tail you could comb.

After we had seen Gwynne and Jock, June and I would join JC in the South of France. The

Riviera was at its sunniest and buzziest in July, when we had the rains in Kenya. JC liked to do things in style. We stayed at the Hotel du Cap in Antibes, a five-star establishment whose huge and extremely fashionable pool and restaurant complex, known as Eden Roc, was described in a yellowing clipping in my old scrapbook as a Riviera playground for international society'. This was the Thirties and, set down among the international jet set, June was in her element. Wide-legged trousers to complement the men's Oxford bags were the ultimate fashion and June, her hair freshly coiffed and bleached, stalked around in the latest pyjamas in the brightest of shades.

If we did not stay in Antibes we would choose Cannes, where we either stayed at the Hotel Miramar or in a private villa. One JC rented several times was called the Chalet and on one occasion Princess Elizabeth, now the Queen, and her sister Princess Margaret Rose were our next-door neighbours. They used to come out on the roof to take the air. I thought them very stuck-up and used to stick my tongue out when I saw them. But they behaved like proper princesses and never reacted.

When we stayed at the Chalet we used to go to the Casino, where there was an Olympic-sized swimming pool. JC's method of teaching me to swim at the age of six was to throw me in the deep end. I was really frightened, petrified I would drown. He, of course, was indifferent. 'You bloody well swim or get a hiding,' was his offer. To keep afloat I instinctively did a sort of dog stroke. Later that same summer he got a coach to teach me the Australian crawl. This wa not for my own fulfilment but so that he could race me against other older children. He would bet 200 francs on my winning. As I got ready he would remind me that if I didn't win I would ge a 'bloody good hiding'. But my worst terror were reserved for the immense diving-board tha towered over the pool at the Casino. 'I'll bet you the brat will go off the top board,' JC would boast to the assembled company. I found diving terrifying. I would stand on the top board blubbering and whimpering . . . The fall seemed to take for ever and I used to hurt my back as I hit the water. But JC won his bet and that was al that mattered.

One day when it was, as usual, blazing hot, I asked for a drink and was told I couldn't have one. I went for a swim and when I came back I found a drink in a tall glass with a straw and sugar round the rim waiting on my table. It was refreshing and lemony and I glugged it down appreciatively. It was, in fact, a Tom Collins which June had ordered for herself. That day I jumped off the top board without protest.

I might not have resented JC's bullying had I ever seen him set an example of the courage and physical prowess he professed so much admiration for. But his maxim was never 'do as I do' but 'do as I say'. The only time I saw him swim was when he was doing what we called goggling but is now known as snorkelling. He certainly was not the powerful racing swimmer I became. And I never saw him dive. In fact, I never saw him do anything physically taxing. He couldn't even ride a horse. According to him horses were dangerous at both ends and damned uncomfortable in the middle'. I have one photograph of him on my pony with his back to the camera. It is a hilarious picture. He was using her to take him up the steep road that led from the coffee factory to the house at Seremai and even the most unhorsy observer can see that he is sitting there like a sack of potatoes and not riding.

They must have made an odd couple, June and JC. JC worshipped all things American. The United States had been his first choice when looking for a place to settle after his quarrel with his mother. He and my mother had spent time in Florida and California, and had hoped to emigrate to the States. In 1919 JC took out preliminary naturalisation papers in San Francisco but his application for US citizenship was rejected. This is said to have been because he had been caught bootlegging. I have no proof but, in view of the way he used to sell rum and gin distilled in the coffee factory at Nyeri, it seems highly probable. He was bitterly disappointed at not achieving US citizenship, so much so that one of his flying documents falsely claimed that he was an American. The legacy of JC's unrequited love affair with the United States was a self-conscious and rather unconvincing American accent that all who met him remarked on and a predilection for American modes. He usually referred to June as 'Junie baby' or 'my baby', used 'automobile' for 'car' and 'phonograph' for 'gramophone'. He even wore American-style underpants, which he insisted on referring to as 'trunks'.

Neither June nor JC was a great intellectual and even their somewhat pedestrian reading matter was American-inspired. June devoured the *Saturday Evening Post*, an American fashion and gossip weekly along the lines of *Hello!*. JC who all his life was fascinated by gangsters and hard men (another reason, perhaps, why bootlegging attracted him), was a regular subscriber to *True Detective*, poring over its line-ups of criminal 'mug shots'.

It was while we were on holiday in the South of France that June gave me my first beating. We were renting the Chalet where there was a black cat, which I liked to take to bed with me. June found out and forbade me to have the creature in my room. I obeyed — albeit reluctantly. A few days later they found cat mess under my bed. It must have gone in there without my knowing and got shut in. I was accused of disobedience — compounded, when I denied it, by lying. June made me pull my knickers down and beat me with a shoe tree. It was excruciating. It had a spring in it which drew blood and left horrendous marks.

Punishment was a regular part of my life as a child. It took various forms. Often I would be locked in my room, sometimes for several days deprived of regular meals. There were other more bizarre punishments. June could be vindictive in an unpredictable way, punishing me for things I didn't even know were transgressions. I had used a gun from an early age shooting pigeons for the pot with my mother's old .22 rifle. One day I shot a crow. When I showed it to June she was annoyed. 'You killed it. You bloody well eat it.' No one eats crow because it's carrion. The Africans hated preparing it for me. The meat stank so. From then on I only killed for the pot.

I was also beaten regularly, though I doubt that either June or JC had been hit themselves as children. I did not resent the beatings *per se*. I don't think, if a child has been really naughty, a hiding does any harm. But like most children I had a well-developed sense of justice. I was prepared to accept punishment if I had done something which deserved it but I did resent the many unfair ones. These were the result either of being disbelieved when I was telling the truth, or of being framed by sadistic adults. It was June who beat me. JC used to take delight in a form of mental torture by frightening me with the threat of a beating, but he never hit me himself. June, who lost her temper easily, used whatever came to hand.

She once accused me of taking a pair of curved nail scissors and cutting up her sheets with them. She produced the sheets, which did, indeed, reveal cuts with a curved outline. Such an idea would never have occurred to me and I denied it. June refused to believe me and was terribly angry. I was terrified and rushed round to Nellie Trench for support. Her advice was to confess. 'But I didn't do it,' I cried over and over again, my sense of justice outraged. 'I can't admit to something I didn't do.' Nothing would convince June that I was telling the truth. I was locked in my room for several days.

Being endlessly landed with someone else's child must be tiresome. I was used to running on a very long rein and June just wanted to have a good time. On occasion her relaxed attitude to supervision verged on disaster. She was friendly with the Hamilton Gordon brothers who ran the racing stables at Nanyuki, where there was a racehorse registered in my name. Their sister Dot married Micky Lyons and built a beautiful house, which is now the very up-market Aberdare Country Club from where all the Treetops safaris start. We had gone up there on a visit when I was about seven. June was chatting to the owner of the stables when I noticed a horse which was muzzled and had a wooden bar across the top of its stable. I have always adored horses and, feeling sorry for him, I went in, took off his muzzle and fed him some carrots. Suddenly the grown-ups missed me and began calling my name.

'Here I am,' I called back, putting out my head.

Total panic followed. I was ordered to come out as quickly and quietly as possible. The horse was a stallion and a killer. He had already kicked and bitten a groom to death.

But some of the trouble I encountered in life was not simply of my own making. June's distaste for stepmotherhood was such that when she was cruising for men and had me in tow she used to introduce me as her kid sister, evidently afraid that the stepmother tag would diminish

86

her pulling power. Ageing and unsexy, that's what being a stepmother was to her. Looking back, I find the role she played in my life was sisterly rather than motherly. But there are sisters and sisters. June Carberry's version was the irresponsible, conspiratorial, controlling type, rather than the protective, affectionate sort.

6

Teaching Chickens to Fly

When I turned seven someone decided it was time I went to school. The departure of Girlie must have had something to do with it. Having nursed me from a few weeks, she left to marry Stephen Parker, the manager of the Standard Bank in Nyeri. But I suspect Granny had a hand in it. My other cousins had been having regular lessons with Mam'selle for a couple of years and it must have been obvious that I would never get to grips with the three Rs if the only contact I had with them was on visits to Riverside Lodge. Besides, as the years went by, visits to Granny grew less frequent. I imagine relations between my grandmother and JC cooled after he married June. June and Granny must have been like chalk and cheese.

My first school was a little private establishment run by a Mrs Henderson, who also ran a coffee farm at Mweiga close to Nyeri. I went as a weekly boarder and used to ride over to Mrs Henderson's house on Monday morning on a mule. When I arrived I would untack her, keep the tack with me and then give the animal a smack on the backside to send her home. Gatimu used to pick me up on Friday in the car.

Mrs Henderson had a son called Ian who was about my age and we used to get up to mischief

together. We would go on to African *shambas*
('*shamba*' means your own private plot) and
steal mealies (corn on the cob). Then we would
go to other African huts to roast them. It didn't
seem ethical to us to roast the mealies in the
same place we had stolen them. Ian was a great
shot and later became a local hero for his stand
against the Mau Mau. His gun got him into
trouble when I knew him. He saw something
moving and assumed it was a buck. It turned out
to be an African child whom he had shot in the
eye.

I stayed at the Hendersons' for a couple of
terms and then was moved to another private
establishment, this time in Nanyuki, which was
some thirty-five miles from Seremai. The new
school, which was called Otakilima (this means
mountain in Kikuyu) was run by a woman called
Jean Ryrie, whose husband Bruce was a farmer. I
was driven there by Gatimu in the car. As JC was
away so often it was decided that I would stay
there full-time without coming home at week-
ends like the other pupils. My sojourn here was
once again to prove limited, due to what were
regarded by the staff and the other pupils as my
wild, gypsy-like — and thoroughly un-European
— ways. It was said by Mrs Ryrie that I didn't
fit in'. For a start, I refused to wear shoes and
insisted on going barefoot. Then there was the
vexed question of hats. Most Europeans wore
hats all the time — usually ghastly topees.
Children were believed to be particularly
vulnerable and went about with squares of red
flannel sewn on to the backs of their topees to

protect their shoulders. There were exceptions to this. Nellie Trench never wore a hat and neither did June or JC. June Carberry loved to be brown and JC took the view that wearing hats in the sun was 'a load of bloody nonsense'. Far from being obliged to wear a hat, I wasn't allowed to. I didn't agree with most of JC's views but I had no problem with that one. My hatless state caused consternation among European adults wherever I went. On one occasion when I was on a ship sailing for England with June Carberry, an old man, seeing me without a hat, warned me that the sun would melt my brains, which would run out of my head through my nose. Whenever I had a cold after that I would wonder whether my brains were seeping away as he had prophesied.

It was while I was at the Ryrie school that JC performed one of his rare altruistic acts. Jean Ryrie's husband Bruce was chopping up meat for his dogs (we didn't have canned pet food then) when he cut himself. The wound turned septic and in no time he was seriously ill with septicaemia. The nearest hospital was in Nairobi, three hours' drive away by road. JC flew him to the Maïa Carberry Nursing Home (which had been founded as a memorial to my mother) in his plane, though sadly not in time to save his life.

I was quite happy to stay at school full-time as I was growing increasingly afraid of JC whose loud, angry voice dominated life at Seremai and whose cruelty repelled me. Whatever I did or said provoked explosions of anger — 'shut up,

90

'brat' or 'why are you so bloody stupid?'. Like all colonials, he made a religion of listening to the news on the BBC World Service at nine o'clock each night, when the power came on down at the factory. He would sit on the sofa in the drawing-room, cigarette held idiosyncratically between his thumb and forefinger, so that he could flick the ash off with his little finger, ear glued to the wireless which, because he was so pro-American, he called the radio. If I dared to speak during this ritual he would bellow, 'Shut up. Can't you see the news is on?'

I shared no interests with JC. His passion — flying — has zero glamour for me. My distaste stems from flying in two-seater planes with him. Whenever he and June went anywhere and took me with them 'the brat' went in with the luggage. It was very unpleasant — pitch dark and claustrophobic, like travelling in the boot of a car. When you got out your limbs had gone to sleep and when they woke up you got pins and needles. Once, June and JC had come back from visiting friends, got straight into a car and drove off, forgetting all about me. I banged and shouted but no one heard. It was not until hours later, when the houseboys and my governess came to push the plane into the hanger, that I was discovered.

Casual jottings about oneself can be surprisingly revealing. In my autograph book, asked his favourite country, JC wrote 'USA'. His favourite book? (I asked this in 1940) '*Mein Kampf.*' His favourite film? '*G-men*', which is shorthand for 'gunmen' — or films about gangsters. Several of the other answers reveal a preoccupation with money. 'What do you want to do when you leave school?' 'Make $ugar' [sic]. 'What do you fear most?' 'Being 'broke'.'

The violence in his nature took the form of cruelty towards vulnerable creatures unable to defend themselves — and that meant me and the animals. I could be intimidated by the threat of beatings, but when it came to the crunch I was quite brave and he couldn't go on beating me for ever. Hurting me through the animals, who, in that rather lonely world, were my best friends, was a subtler game.

One evening when I was about eight he cooked up a plan to 'teach the chicken to fly'. 'I know what we'll do. We'll take it up in an aeroplane.' And he did. I was there when the chicken came down. The poor thing was dazed and disorientated but it lived to tell the tale. The kitten was not so lucky. Down at the factory there was a heavy-duty floor-mounted centrifugal drill with two big balls, which acted as weights and hung down when the drill was not in use. When it was turning, the balls swung out and up. One day when I was there, helping to pack the coffee into the Cellophane packets or bent on getting myself a tinful of the delicious sugar cane juice as it poured out from the crusher, JC grabbed a little black kitten, tied it on to the T-shaped arm of the drill and started it up. Round and round it spun in front of my horrified gaze until, as a result of the violence of the centrifugal force, its head burst and the ground was covered in blood and brains. JC's esponse was roars of delight.

I was nine when, rapture of raptures, I was deemed old enough to have my own pony. Since the days when I used to be led around on Mafuta, my mother's old pony, I had always adored horses and spent hours in the stables grooming Nellie Trench's pony Simba and the mules which all farmers in Africa used. After much badgering on my part JC had given way. Lelly (her real name was 'Lady' but the Africans couldn't pronounce that) was a neat grey Somali pony who cost £5. She was evil incarnate and JC had only bought her because he thought she would savage me and put me off being horsy for life. Lelly had horrible habits and I was terrified of riding her. She would buck and buck to get you off. If that failed she would get down and roll on you. But though she was a Jezebel to ride, in the stable she was as gentle as a lamb. I had always wanted long flowing hair but JC would never allow me to grow mine, so I transferred all my yearning for swirling tresses to my pony and used to spend hours in the stable with her, grooming her coat and combing and combing the beautiful silky tail that reached almost to the ground. In Africa, of course, this tail was not just a pretty adornment. It was vital to keep away the clouds of marauding insects that plagued the livestock.

JC had a boat down at the coast and used to like deep-sea fishing. Many of the fish he was after — barracuda, kingfish, marlin, tunny — were wary of taking the hook and he preferred to entice the fish using lures which were made of

white horse-hair dyed in vivid colours. One day
went into Lelly's stable to groom her as usua
and found her once-beautiful tail just a shorr
stump. Appalled and tearful, I rushed tc
confront JC to ask him what he had done tc
Lelly. He found my distress hilarious. 'They
make bloody good lures,' was his only comment
Poor Lelly. She was covered in flies for ages aftei
that and her tail never recovered its former glory
remaining ragged and uneven.

Children, like animals, are extremely sensitive
to evil and most of the children who knew JC
feared him as I did. My cousins, Peter and Patty
Anderson, went into the bedroom at Serema
one day when they were staying at Nyeri. JC
liked Patty, a pretty little girl whom he used tc
call 'Cutie', in his pseudo-American voice. Mucl
to the distress of Patty, who was protective
towards her brother, JC told her she could stay
but roared at a terrified Peter to get out as he
was 'no use at all'. Patty saw him at Malindi or
the coast a few years later when she was about
eleven and had grown rather plump. 'You're nc
longer Cutie,' he sneered. 'You're just a fai
lump.'

It was soon after the kitten incident that I
discovered I had another Granny. When JC's
mother Mary Carberry came to Kenya she
didn't stay at Seremai, which even as a child I
thought was odd. Instead, I went to see her. She
was staying with her second husband, Kit
Sandford, in a small, isolated cottage up-country
where the ice-cool streams team with trout. I
have only hazy memories of that visit. The

cottage, which was a one-storey building, constructed of cedar wood so the termites wouldn't eat it, was totally isolated. When you looked out from the veranda, where I sat with Granny and Kit, who had a shock of white hair, you could see no other humanity, just Africa.

As a child I didn't know that JC had had a volcanic quarrel with his mother or that he had once been Lord Carberry and master of a Gothic castle far away in Ireland. Now that I have discovered more about our family history it seems likely that Granny made the trip to Africa to try to bury the hatchet with her eldest son. I don't know that JC even saw her. He wasn't with us the day I visited.

Was there a sexual element in JC's unpleasantness? Modern wisdom has it that those who display violence have experienced it in their formative years. I doubt that this was the case with JC. His mother certainly had the most indulgent of upbringings with a kindly, philanthropic father and an adoring nanny who was full of loving common sense. She wrote of her own childhood in *Happy World*, 'We are never whipped or slapped, partly because we are good children, too happy to be naughty, and partly because Nanny thinks punishments do more harm than good.'

It is possible that JC was impotent, or at least had sexual difficulties. I never saw him show any sign of sexual interest in June or anyone else, which might go some way to explain June's apparently insatiable appetite for casual coupling. A conversation which has stuck in my

mind was a discussion I overheard between June
and JC on the subject of something called
monkey gland. The intriguing expression caused
my young ears to prick up, even though I had no
idea what it meant, and I suspect the clarity of
my memory indicates that I heard the expression
more than once at Seremai. It was many years
before I discovered that monkey gland was the
Thirties answer to Viagra. JC never beat me
himself but liked to be there when someone else
did. There may even have been a voyeuristic
element in his relationship with June. People
who knew them say that she occasionally
entertained a boyfriend overnight at Seremai
when JC was there and that, far from being put
out, JC used to join them for breakfast in June's
bedroom. If this is true it might explain why she
took so little trouble to conceal her infidelities
and why, despite them, the Carberrys had an
enduring marriage.

7

Spirits of the Baobab

Most summers, when I hadn't been made to spend my holidays at boarding-school, I went with Maxwell and Nellie Trench to their seaside house Jadini at Diani. Jadini was an affectionate tribute to their three children Jack, Anne (who was always called Nancy) and Dan, '*ini*' means place of' in Swahili, making Jadini 'the place of Jack, Anne and Dan'. This was just over twenty miles south of Mombasa on the Indian Ocean and meant a five-day trip by road through Tanganyika. Today it is the National Park but then it was still a wilderness. August was the rainy season and the weather up-country was cold and grey, and horrid at that time. At the coast, on the other hand, it was always balmy — even at night when everyone slept on their verandas to try to keep cool. I loved the trip, which meant several nights camping safari-style in the bush. We would set off from Seremai in a convoy of three or four vehicles including a lorry which would be driven by the *watu* — the Swahili word for people, generally used to mean Africans — containing all the camping stuff. Just before sundown we would stop to make camp and Dan, the Trenches' youngest son, and I would be sent off into the bush to collect firewood, or *kuni*, while the boys put up the tents. Cooking was done over a campfire which heated the makeshift 'stove' — in reality three big stones. Then the *sufuria*, or cooking pot, was put on to boil. The next priority was to protect the supplies from what the Africans called *dudus*. *Dudu* is a generic term for insect, but the chief enemy to anyone camping in the bush are the *siafu*, or safari ants. They are sinister, yet fascinating creatures, who march in vast disciplined columns so long you could never see the beginning or the end. They could get in through any aperture, however small and, once in, like miniature panzer tanks, they kept on coming in wave after wave, devouring anything in their path, including living flesh. If they got into the poultry house or the rabbit hutch, where the animals couldn't get away from them, you would find your livestock dead in the morning. If they invaded the stables you would hear the horses stamping and kicking, and screaming in terror. All you could do was open the door and let them out. Stories were even told of colonial mothers who had left their babies outside for a sleep, safe, as they thought, under a nice net so that the *dudus* would not eat them, had heard them crying, decided to let them cry for a while, only to discover, when they went to bring them in, half-eaten corpses covered in safari ants. Death is caused by suffocation as the ants go in through orifices — ears, nostrils and, in the case of babies, open bawling mouths. Water is no barrier. The soldier ants, who travel at the side of the column and are bigger, throw themselves in and make a bridge for the others to cross over

The one thing that deters them is paraffin. On safari the provisions travelled in a meat safe with wire mesh walls. When we stopped to make camp each of the four legs of the safe would be placed in a metal dish containing paraffin. Mothers would place the legs of their babies' cots in dishes topped up with it for the same reason.

Fearsome though they could be, safari ants had a sophisticated and intriguing method of communication. When I came across a marching column as a child — they used to come out in the rains and you would see them lying across the road like a great dark snake — I used to pick a soldier ant and tease him. Somehow he told all the other ants because in no time they would leave the column and rush to his aid in fighting the enemy. The same bush telegraph could be seen at work whenever a human inadvertently found himself among safari ants. They would invade in fairly large numbers — they were constantly swarming up men's trouser legs — but they wouldn't bite straight away. Suddenly one of the ants would give the signal — 'now lads!' — and they'd bite together and all hell would break loose.

Europeans were wary of safari ants but if you cut yourself in the bush the Africans had a way of turning them into highly efficient suture material. They would catch one ant and get him to bite the two sides of the cut towards each other. As he brought his mandibles together the African would deftly snap the body from the head, leaving the head to act as a very clean, neat suture.

Even when we were on safari there was no real question of roughing it. As usual, the boys waited on us hand and foot — the only reason Dan and I fetched the firewood was that we liked going off into the bush. We were intrigued by the creatures we might find there. Once we came upon a hyena and chased it. We weren't scared of lions. They are more afraid of us than we are of them. The only animal we were a bit worried about walking into was the rhino. In those days they were numerous and they are unpredictable creatures, aggressive even towards each other and prone to charging at whatever they see.

Night-time in the bush in those days was magical. The stars in the African night sky are so prolific — a hundred times more so than in any sky you ever see in Europe — that they give off their own light, an effect intensified by the fact that there was no electric light to compete with it. It was Maxwell Trench who first showed me the Southern Cross, which can only be seen in skies south of the Equator and which we found most nights. It was he who taught me how to identify the planet Venus, which in African skies burns with a greenish hue, and Mars whose light is red.

Maxwell, who had always lived in hot climates, was a mine of arcane knowledge. He was particularly good on home medicine, a vital skill in a huge country where distances between towns are considerable. He'd kept his father's log-book from Jamaica, which contained all sorts of remedies. When we were injured he would tell us that in the West Indies, where an infection often led to nasty ulcers called yaws, they used to bandage a couple of cockroaches — or maggots — into an open sore. Apparently they would eat up all the pus and clean the wound absolutely beautifully. Europeans think this is disgusting but the fact is that although cockroaches are found in dirty places the dirt is invariably created by humans. What's more, no one knows of a disease that has been spread by cockroaches.

On safari in the bush the night sounds were a magical concert. Once we children had turned out the hurricane lamps and were tucked up in our camp-beds we would listen in wonder to those mysterious and fascinating noises, quite different by night from by day. In the daytime we often heard the rumble of contented elephant conversation — happy elephants make a pleasant sound like a loud purr — the snort of an impala scenting danger, or the loud barking of baboons. But at night we would identify the grunt of a prowling lion, the strange hiccuping of a startled zebra — like a donkey uttering the hee on an in-drawn breath, without the haw — the blood-curdling shriek of a hyrax.

Sometimes, to my delight, we drove on after nightfall. I loved driving in the dark because of the eyes that our headlights lit up, mysterious, glittering and revealing a tantalising glimpse of a secret nocturnal world not meant to be seen by us. Sometimes it would be one eye — that would be a spring hare, whose eyes are set far back in its head so that you rarely see two at the same time; occasionally a pair would jump in the air in front of us — that would be a nightjar, a heavy, lazy bird the size of a big pigeon who likes to lie on the sun-warmed road until the last possible minute; mostly they were green — serval cats, lions, antelopes, hyenas and jackals, and occasionally a reddish eye high up from the ground revealed the presence of elephants.

I feel privileged to have known Diani before the world discovered it. Go to this sought-after coastal resort today and you will find a beach of snow-white sand backed by a mass of concrete that seems to be trying to shove the beach back into the sea. It is so urban you could be in Rio de Janeiro, with a violent crime problem to match that of any South American city. The hotels, all with their private swimming pools, for tourists fear the teeming life that roams the tropical waters of the Indian Ocean, crowd in together as if convinced that safety lies in numbers. One of the smartest is the Hotel Jadini. The beach is crammed with sunbathing bodies in every shade from angry carmine to deep bronze.

The Diani of my childhood resembled the undiscovered shore of Daniel Defoe's magic island, with me and Dan Trench playing the parts of Robinson Crusoe and Man Friday. With its dazzling white coral sand leading down to a peacock-blue ocean it was the tropical paradise that travel brochures endlessly promise but rarely deliver. The excitement in the car as we reached the end of our long journey reached fever pitch as we played the fiercely contested game of 'who's going to see the sea first?'. In those days there were one or two little coast hotels with palm thatch or *makuti* roofs, but you hardly ever saw anybody on the beach. Jadini, Maxwell Trench's house, was two or three unassuming flat-roofed buildings which he was continually adding to as we grew out of the modest original, adding first a separate kitchen and dining-room, then a bar, then a place for billiard and ping-pong tables . . .

Diani was a place where nature was sublime. The Trenches, unlike the Carberrys, were early risers, so we savoured together one of the most visually intoxicating treats Africa has to offer. Daybreak at the coast is spectacular. There is no wind at this time and the sea is as still as glass. Suddenly, like a golden orb, the sun begins to rise out of the sea and as it does so it turns the water all around it to liquid gold.

The dense, green, mysterious forest began a matter of yards from the house. It was full of wildlife. There were bush-babies, mongooses, delightful Jackson's chameleons with three horns and monkeys of all kinds which chattered constantly — black and white colobus monkeys, vervet monkeys, sykes and baboons. The dogs hated the monkeys and would bark at them constantly. But the last thing you wanted was for the dogs to kill one. If they attacked a baboon or a sykes — and this happened from time to time — you could expect a Mafia-like vendetta. The monkey troop would turn out in force for vengeance and the dog would be ripped to pieces.

Drifting above us on huge pied wings we would often see the magnificent fish eagle whose distinctive, haunting cry spells Africa to so many of us exiles. There were also leopards in the forest. They used to come after the goats. They'd put their paws through the enclosure and literally tear bits off them, so that the night air would sometimes be rent with the goats' screams. When there were leopards about we would get up in the morning and find the pens full of lacerated dead and dying goats. In retaliation we would set traps, vicious iron leg-hold traps and when a leopard was caught someone would take a gun and go out and shoot it.

Our days at Diani revolved around the sea: swimming, snorkelling and surfing. Dan and I used to love racing hermit crabs. We would take two sticks and tie a piece of string to each of them. One end would go into the sand and the other would trace a big circle. Then we would go off and hunt for the crabs. A small shell moving unaccountably across the sand was a sure sign it was inhabited. Of course, they're very timid and as soon as you pick up the shell they retreat inside using their big nipper claw as a front door. I discovered that if you blow on them they come out but you have to keep your fingers out of the way or they'll have you — and they really hang on. When we had found about a dozen crabs we would mark their shells with numbers, using old stamp papers, and put them under an inverted tin. The grown-ups would be summoned and invited to place their bets. Maxwell was a very enthusiastic gambler. At last the tin would be removed and the crabs would be off amid much shouting and yelling. Because you can't persuade crabs to travel in a straight line the first one to cross the circle would be declared the winner.

Nancy was my surfing partner. There is a coral reef off the coast on which crash snowy-white breakers. We would wait till midway between high and low tide, because that was when you got the biggest breakers, and swim right out beyond the reef to get the big ones. You only ever got about three good surfs in a session because it was such a struggle to get out through the breakers to where the big ones broke. It was perfect because at the end, instead of washing you up on to a beach, the waves broke gently on to the reef and landed you there waist deep, ready to set out again to ride the next one.

The beach was so deserted that a friend of ours called Keith Campling, who ran an air taxi company called Campling and Vanderwal, used to land his plane on it. It had to be low tide as the sand above the high-water mark was too soft. But there were sinky patches where it was soft on the exposed sand too, so he had to be careful. The drill was that Keith would appear and zoom low over the beach. That was the signal for us to take up our positions. We were to stand on the soft bits to warn him not to land there. One year Keith took Nancy and me up in his plane and flew over the reef. There, swimming about where we loved to surf, were half a dozen big sharks. I don't recall Nancy and me being so keen on surfing after that.

One of my great delights at Diani was to go out fishing with the Africans. About half a mile offshore is a great coral reef which runs the whole length of the Kenyan coast, broken now and again by openings called *mlangos* through which boats can pass. Every day the African fishermen would go out with the tide in their *ngalawa* — dug-out canoes, equipped with outriggers to prevent them capsizing — to fish on the reef. Sometimes they would take me with them and teach me how to catch octopus using pointed sticks. What you did was walk along the reef looking out for holes in the coral. Octopuses like to hide in these holes, concealing the entrance with stones. If you found such a stone you pulled it. If it pulled back you knew someone was home. You then took a thin pliable stick and poked it into the hole. The idea was to irritate the octopus. After a while he gets so fed up he attacks, wrapping his tentacles round the stick — and your arm. You have to train yourself not to recoil or resist until his body is well out of the hole. Then you grab the body. You have to act fast. Octopuses are equipped with a black bony weapon like a parrot's beak, which can give a very painful bite. As soon as you have hold of the body you rip the tentacles off your arm, turn the body inside out and beat the octopus on a rock to kill it. If I caught one I would take it back to the kitchen *totos* who would cook it for me.

When the tide was in, the Africans used to catch fish on the reef with spears. It was they who taught me what was dangerous and venomous in the tropical sea. The reef was one place where I never went barefoot, though the Africans did. I always wore *takkis* — what you would call trainers today — or native football boots which protected the ankle. The coral was very sharp and there were too many sea urchins, stonefish, scorpion fish and sting-rays. There were rarely sharks: though they were able to come in at high tide they were very conscious that they could be stranded.

It was through the fishermen at Diani that I discovered the *shaitani*. JC loathed anything to do with religion. This stemmed from the feud with his mother. His hatred of Christianity had a positive spin-off for me. At all the schools he chose I was excused religious instruction. There was, therefore, a vacuum in my heathen soul and into this vacuum came the *shaitani*. All my life I have had a great respect for African witchcraft. Africans subscribe to the God-in-Nature view of the world and *shaitani* are the spirits who inhabit places like caves and trees — particularly baobabs and banyans — and who must be appeased by man. I was always more aware of the presence of *shaitani* and the witch-doctors who communicated with them at the coast than up-country. Without offerings, the spirits can be very spiteful. Never mess with them, the Africans told me. To indicate that a particular tree or cave was inhabited by spirits the witch-doctor, or *mganga*, used to tie pieces of red or white cloth to sticks and plant the sticks in prominent places. Baobabs often have big cavities and you would find offerings of food or coins left in them. When I went out on the reef with the fishermen they would always appease the *shaitani* who lived in the caves to ensure that we came safely home.

Several Europeans were building houses on the beach when I was a child. They often used to bring *fundi* or builders down with them from up-country as they were less superstitious, but whenever they ploughed ahead without the necessary appeasements they fell or injured themselves. Maxwell Trench got involved with the *shaitani* when he was building Jadini. There were coral cliffs there and he wanted to extend his house. None of the local builders would agree, saying the spirits would not approve. Maxwell got angry and said he would blow the *shaitani* out of the rocks with dynamite. He did so and a piece of rock flew out and severed the artery in his leg. The Africans just nodded and said, 'We told you so.' When they insisted that the witch-doctor must be sent for and that a black goat had to be sacrificed Maxwell was forced to go along with it. A black goat was likewise required before digging a well. Without it the well would be found to contain salt water.

As a child I accepted unquestioningly what the Africans told me about their magic — but strange things happened to me after I grew up, too. In the forest down at the coast there was an enormous baobab tree. I had known it all my life. When we came back from fishing trips the Africans would navigate by it so that they could find their way through the *mlango*. The monkeys used to like cracking open the large seeds and sucking out the thirst-quenching juice inside which tasted like cream of tartar, and so did I. Because it was growing on dead coral the tree had spread its roots mostly above ground. They fanned out all around it standing a good foot above the earth so that little children like me could walk the tightrope on them. It was regarded as a holy tree by the Africans. Long after I was grown up and had joined the Merchant Navy I was telling some friends from a Dutch ship about the baobab tree. We set off in search of it. But, no matter where I looked, I couldn't find it. Nor was there any space where it had been. I was deeply puzzled. The next time I went out to the reef with the fishermen I asked what had happened to the *shaitani* tree.

'Nothing,' they said.

'But I took some people to see it and I couldn't find it.'

The fishermen roared with laughter. 'Of course you couldn't. They didn't believe in it. You were showing it to non-believers. It's there all right.'

And it is. Preserved, I am happy to say, in the grounds of one of Diani's big hotels.

8

Swimming with Sharks

John Carberry also had a place on the coast — at Malindi, eighty miles north of Mombasa. But whereas a trip to Diani with the Trenches was an essentially African experience, travelling with the Carberrys never lost that detached, slightly effete feel of the rich colonial. For a start, June and JC never camped. In time, JC had his own airstrip built at Malindi, which meant we could travel from Nyeri in the most luxurious manner of all. But in the beginning we took the night train from Nairobi to Mombasa, which left the city at six o'clock at night and arrived at the coast at eight the next morning. We used to load June's Ford V8 on the back.

Compared with the functional trains of today the old sleepers of the imperial era were as comfortable as five-star hotels. The cabins were two- or four-berth, equipped with wash-basins and fans. Drinks and early-morning tea could be summoned at the press of a bell; lavatories, which were a short walk down the corridor, came in two types — sit-upon European and squat-down Asian — and there were three sittings for dinner, sold on a ticket basis and announced by a steward who walked the length of the train beating out a simple tune on an instrument which resembled a small portable xylophone. The tune, reminiscent of those sing-song appeals itinerant ice-cream vans use to attract children, was known as the Officers' Dinner Call. While you ate in the dining-car (the food was delicious), the steward made up the beds. For a small supplement you could have a mattress, a perk JC always took advantage of. I had to make do with the seat. All the staff — cooks, waiters, stewards — were Goan, the consequence of hundreds of years of domination of the East African coast by the Portuguese. The windows in the cabins could be raised or lowered using a strap to secure the pane at the desired height. As we pulled out of Nairobi we always left the window down as there was invariably game to be seen on the Athi Plains. As soon as it started to get dark, we pulled up a wire mesh screen to keep out the malaria-carrying mosquitoes that infest the coastal area and the soot from the train smoke.

To reach Mombasa, which is an island, the train had to cross the Makupa Causeway. From the station we usually made our way to the southern end of the island where June liked to refresh herself after the train journey at one of the landmarks of old Mombasa, the Manor Hotel. This was a lovely rambling building with a touch of old-fashioned luxury about it, despite its roof of green-washed corrugated iron. It dated back to the earliest pioneering days of the turn of the century.

The most charming part of Mombasa was the old port. It was here, towards the end of the year when the *kaskazi* monsoon blows from the

111

north-east, that the graceful dhows would sail in, laden with the sort of cargoes they have been transporting for thousands of years: beautiful objects from the Arabian gulf and sea — Persian carpets, elaborately worked Arab chests, Mangalore roofing tiles from India — and foodstuffs — sacks of Egyptian cotton seed for cattle feed, dried fruit, dried and salted fish . . . Here, on a low coral cliff commanding the harbour, was Mombasa's oldest monument, the pink-washed Moorish-style fortress of Fort Jesus, built at the end of the sixteenth century to subdue the area's hostile Arabs. In my day it was a prison run by the British where, a few years hence, John Carberry would serve time. Almost next door was the exclusive Mombasa Club, for which all British officers were eligible. Membership was particularly sought after as it had its own sea water swimming pool.

To reach Malindi from Mombasa we left the island via the Nyali bridge and headed north. Today the Nyali bridge is a fixed structure built of concrete but in my childhood it was one of the longest pontoon bridges in the world. The early part of the drive took us through the Vipingo sisal estate, which extended for miles. Sisal was a huge industry in those days, when British farmers used nothing else to tie up their hay and straw. The thing I always noticed was that although the land had been cleared for growing sisal the baobab trees were left standing. I doubt whether the adults knew why, but I did: it was because of the *shaitani*. Soon after this we came to the creek at Kilifi which had to be crossed by ferry. This was one of the highlights of the journey. Today you drive across a bridge but in the Thirties you put the car on a chain ferry. The Africans pulled it across by walking backwards hauling on the chain. As they worked they sang and stomped, accompanying themselves by blowing on conch shells. They sang in Swahili and their songs were about whatever they saw around them. Very often they featured their unsuspecting European passengers. A bald head, an unkempt beard, a pair of rather large breasts would be spotted and woven into an extempore and not particularly respectful celebration — much to the glee of one small Swahili-speaking European child.

North of Kilifi the road entered the Sokoke-Arabuko forest. This was the best bit of the journey. On the narrow dusty track which bisected the seething green jungle you often saw elephants. In the forest grew tall majestic tropical trees — ebony, teak, *mbambakofi* and *mvuli* (both tropical hardwoods) — and on them, in the jostling exuberance of fertility unleashed by the dense, humid air, romped creepers, ferns and orchids. Above our heads flew black and white colobus monkeys while on the ground we'd see giant slow-moving monitor lizards, all kinds of antelope — the tiny suni dik-dik, duiker, bush buck — and the occasional leopard. This forest was home to the rare little Sokoke Scops owl. We often used to hear its strange call, not the 'toowit toowoo' of British owls, but a strange 'tonk tonk tonk'. I wonder how long it will survive now. Tragically the forest has been cut down. What used to be a narrow track leading through a garden of Eden that sheltered dozens of species of trees, flowers, animals, birds and reptiles, is now a wide tarmac road flanked on either side by a cosmetic strip of forest a few yards wide. In the rains, when everything is green, it still looks quite dense, but in the drought you can look straight through and see how soon it ends and cultivated land starts.

At the northern end of Malindi Bay was the mouth of the Sabaki river. At night JC used to take us up there with a spotlight to shoot crocodiles. We'd pick out their eyes with the torch and take pot-shots at them. It was such a waste of life. We did not even get the skins as if you shoot a croc in water it sinks.

Even in my childhood Malindi was more developed than Diani. This part of the coast was colonised by the Arabs in the Middle Ages. It had been a Phoenician port in the ancient world and had been run first by the Portuguese and latterly by the Arabs. Of course, it was nothing like the seething mass of charmless beach hotels it has since become. Today it even boasts a golf course. In my childhood, in addition to the *bandas*, or beach houses, such as ours, there were two old hotels, Lawfords and the Sinbad. These were built in a style found all over the tropics, with mangrove poles called *boriti* and thatched *makuti* roofs. There was even a shop, a general store run by Mr Abbas, an Arab, where you could buy Omo, Vim, baked beans and newspapers. Another feature, long since vanished, was a camel mill. Under a roof of thatch

114

he unfortunate beast, blindfolded, walked round and round all day grinding millet and *sim sim*, or sesame seed.

The climate at the coast was hot and humid. The temperature at the hottest time of the year, which was December, January and February, was in the high nineties and the humidity was ninety per cent. Because of this all windows and doors that could be opened in a house were flung wide to maximise through-draught. There was often no window glass, just shutters, and doors between rooms were only waist high, like stable doors. A spin-off of this draught-creating architecture was a certain lack of privacy. This was overcome by the immeasurably useful Swahili expression '*hodi*'. This translates as 'may I come in?' and was used by anybody approaching, from the houseboy with the early tea to an unexpected guest in search of a sundowner.

At the coast everyone slept on the veranda, a companionable habit I liked, having always been afraid of the dark on my own. We slept on *usutu* beds. These had a wooden frame, with a kapok-filled mattress (kapok trees grew all along the coast) supported on a base of webbing made of plaited coconut. Each bed was shrouded in its own mosquito net, which hung from a ring in the veranda ceiling. Despite the care we took to prevent ourselves from being bitten, malaria was endemic among Europeans and Africans. Everyone got it. It was regarded as about as serious as flu is now. I have had it so often I've lost count. It took ten days to incubate and when you got it

you would be ill for five. In those days the onl
remedy was horrid, bitter-tasting quinine (th
same quinine that my grandmother used to sto
me sucking my thumb) and lots and lots t
drink. If you didn't drink you would ge
black-water fever, which was serious.

At first the Carberry *banda* was as primitive a
the Trenches' down the coast. Under the *makut*
roof were several bedrooms, with a veranda al
round and a detached kitchen. What I love
about these *makuti* roofs was that they wer
home to any number of uninvited wildlife. The
accommodated lizards, bats and the creature
which preyed on them. It was not unknown for a
snake with its eye on a gecko to lose its footing i
the *makuti* roof and land on somebody, causin
pandemonium. All these creatures had to reliev
themselves and it was quite normal to hear a
splash and observe a small quantity of bat o
gecko guano floating in someone's soup, a
feature which persuaded many Europeans to pu
up ceilings. The geckos, being nocturnal, usuall
spent the day holed up behind the pictures on
the walls, only coming out at night. They woul
make funny 'clic clic clic' noises to each other
Sometimes a fight would break out behind a
picture and you'd see it suddenly leaping aroun
on the wall. The geckos had an unpleasant habi
of pooping on books, but they ate all kinds o
insects and moths, so most people didn't min
them.

Lack of running water meant pit latrines
These were the norm all over East Africa unti
the Blue Posts Hotel at Thika installed the firs

lush lavatories in the colony during the Twenties. Bathing was a problem at the coast. To compensate there was the beach where, unlike at Diani, the sand was sand-coloured and where, because there was no reef at this point, the surf was huge. Ever an early riser, I used to go off with the African *totos* in the early morning to look for turtle eggs on the beach. The eggs had a leathery skin, which you pierced to suck out the inside. Unlike hens' eggs, there was no white, just a delicious rich yolk. The other thing I did as soon as I arrived was hunt out my beloved *madafu*. This was a treat I never experienced up-country. *Madafu* is the juice of an unripe coconut before the flesh has formed and is the most delicious thing you could possibly imagine. The grown-ups used to drink it with gin, which must have been sacrilege. *Madafu* always gave me the squitters, but it was worth it.

While living standards were fairly basic, the Malindi *banda* was a separate establishment from Seremai, with its own staff, headed by Kaimoi, a Kikuyu who had come from up-country. The local staff looked after the livestock: goats who provided us with milk (you could not keep cows or horses at the coast because of the tsetse fly); an ostrich who used to terrorise the boys when they were doing the *dhobi* by stealing the soap and eating it; and various pets — mongooses, bush-babies and an assortment of monkeys. The bush-baby was June's. In reality they make lousy pets. They do sweet things like eat bananas from your hand while perched on your shoulder but then pee

117

down your back as they're doing it. They're also nocturnal. When I wanted to play with them they were flat out and very uninteresting, and at night when I wanted to sleep they would clatter about emitting banshee-like shrieks. People from up-country would often appear at breakfast complaining nervously that there had been something walking about on the roof in the night. Bush-babies were popular pets partly because they looked so appealing with their huge eyes and little human hands, and partly because they were so easy to capture: they feed on the fruit of the cashew-nut tree and sometimes this fruit is fermenting so they get drunk and fall out of the trees. Then the Africans pick them up and sell them.

In addition to the permanent staff we used to bring some of the boys from Nyeri with us as well. Waiganjo usually came, adapting his mechanical skills from planes to boats. The local Africans from the coast north of Mombasa were Giriama whose women go topless, wearing only Hawaiian-style skirts made from strips of calico. Our boys used to watch them goggle-eyed.

Up-country most colonials stuck devoutly to a white man's diet. At the coast, however, the cooking became more African. There was still ham and toast and marmalade for breakfast, but there would also be pawpaws and mangoes. There would be fish and goat curries to replace the English roasts and, most delicious of all, the wonderful staple of Swahili cooking, *tui*. This is a kind of coconut cream made from mixing the grated flesh of the coconut with hot water and

Me at seventeen.

John Carberry as a child in Ireland; and
with his younger brother Ralfe.

Maïa Carberry was the first person to fly non-stop from Mombasa to Nairobi.

John Carberry as a young man. JC hated being photographed and so I hav no pictures of him during my years at Seremai.

A rare shot of me with my mother.

The house at Seremai.

Me with Maxwell Trench.

From left to right: Kamau (who looked after me), Mathenge (the pantry boy), Gatimu (the head houseboy) and Kimani (the cook).

Me with horrid bob
and scratchy dress.

Maxwell Trench.

Nellie Trench.

…he Carberry; *and right* relaxing at Seremai.

…e, aged eleven, with two fellow pupils at finishing school.

Pieter, the Rutt, June and me with the crocodile which was made into a handbag for June.

Travelling by rickshaw in Mombasa, behind the Manor Hotel.

Me and my dog Boppy with Valerie Ward, one of the habitués of June's parties.

Kikuyu witch doctor *(left)* wearing hyrax skin cape.

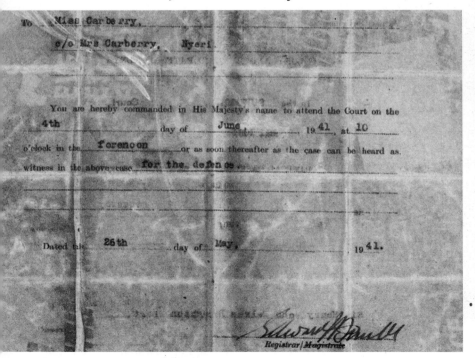

Animals — Horses & Bears
Pastimes — Hunting
Subject — Roman History
Sport — Hunting
Love — Anticipation
Career — Landowner
Book — Mr Pickwick
Country — England
Film — Ben Hur
Fear — Londiners

Jelves Broughton
27.1.41

e autograph book signed by Delves Broughton.
e questions were: what is your favourite
mal/pastime/subject/sport/career/book/country/film;
at is better than love; and what do you fear most?

To   Miss Carberry,
      c/o Mrs Carberry,   Nyeri.

You are hereby commanded in His Majesty's name to attend the Court on the
4th   day of   June,   19 41, at 10
o'clock in the   forenoon   or as soon thereafter as the case can be heard as.
witness in the above case   for the defence.

Dated this   26th   day of   May,   19 41.

                                        Edward H Baull
                                        Registrar/Magistrate

My summons to the Lord Erroll murder trial.

Family picnic with Patty, Aunt Caroline and Uncle Gerald.

Dr Gerald Anderson, my uncle.

Very proud to be FANY.

orcing the resulting liquid through a sieve. It forms the basis of many of the sauces in which ish and other curries are cooked in coastal dishes. The grown-ups used it as a substitute for cream in coffee. I thought it delicious on fruit salads.

As the years went by, the Malindi house, like the Trenches' at Diani, grew in size and sophistication. JC built a club near the house which he called the Eden Roc after his favourite watering hole on the French Riviera. The name survives, though the Eden Roc of today is just another tourist hotel. Another name from my childhood is Ngowe House. This is an old folks' home, but its name describes a type of mango native to Jamaica that Maxwell planted next to JC's Malindi airstrip. The old tree is still there sixty years later.

The building of the Eden Roc Club, which was largely the work of the ever resourceful Maxwell Trench, brought with it running water and flushing lavatories. To reach water they had to sink a borehole, though the water at the coast always tasted brackish. When it came to equipping the cisterns of the lavatories, JC, who was always penny wise and pound foolish, decreed that ball valves were a needless expense. Instead, they would use old bully-beef cans. The labour of first soldering them up and then replacing them, as they rusted up in the water, far outweighed any initial saving.

Just as at Nyeri John Carberry had his planes, at the coast he kept that other toy beloved of rich playboys, his yacht. Luxury boating was an expensive hobby even in those days and JC was one of only a handful of men in the colony who could afford it. JC's boat, *Nguva*, was a luxurious, carpeted motor vessel with a big double cabin and a smaller one where I slept. Today we would call her a gin palace. *Nguva* is the African name for a dugong, or sea-cow, the lethargic mammal native to the Indian Ocean which is believed to have been the inspiration for the mermaid legend. Much of the time we spent at the coast revolved around *Nguva*, which was moored in Mombasa Harbour. It was to equip himself with lures for a deep-sea fishing expedition aboard *Nguva* that JC had cut off the lovely tail of my pony Lelly. He used to take *Nguva* down to Pemba Island north of Zanzibar to fish for tunny, koli koli, marlin and barracuda.

JC may have been a skilled aviator but he wasn't a particularly competent sailor. He never went out on *Nguva* by himself. Maxwell Trench usually acted as navigator, Waiganjo always came in case anything went wrong with the engine and then we invariably had another boy or two on board to do the cooking and cleaning and to gut the fish.

JC liked to go shark fishing. The seas round Mombasa have sharks in plenty. JC would sail *Nguva* round to the northern side of Mombasa island up an inlet known as Tudor Creek, where there was a slaughterhouse. The blood and guts that ran out into the sea attracted the sharks while the slaughterhouse was a convenient source of bait. There JC would put out shark hooks, baited with a sheep's head, with the

120

ubiquitous *debbe* (oil tin) acting as a float. High on one bank overlooking the creek was the Tudor House Hotel where we used to stay, run by a man called White. He had a son who was some years older than me. On one occasion, when I was about twelve, JC insisted that I and this boy race each other 400 yards across Tudor Creek because he wanted to take bets on who would win. Because of the risk of attack by sharks White would only allow his son to take part if a boat accompanied him but JC made no such stipulation for me. He stayed up on the veranda of the hotel while we went down to the beach and launched in. I was terrified and my one thought was to get it over with. We came back in the boat and I don't even remember who won.

The race was not the only time JC forced me to swim in waters he knew to be shark-infested but the next time it happened he got more than he bargained for. *Nguva* was moored in Kilindini Harbour, between the mainland and the south side of Mombasa island in front of the Outrigger Yacht Club, where some divers had already been taken by sharks. Opposite *Nguva*'s moorage was a jetty where there was a fleet of little motor boats operating like a taxi service for people who wanted to go ashore from ships and boats. It was run by a man called Kempton and the boats were known as K boats. In those pre-radio days when you wanted to go ashore you hoisted a special blue-and-yellow K flag and a boat would come out to you.

One day — I must have been about fourteen at the time — JC wanted to go ashore. *Nguva* had her own dinghy but on that occasion it was at K boats about a hundred yards away on the shore. JC told me to swim ashore and bring back the dinghy. Knowing there were sharks in the water I refused — so he threw me in. I swam ashore as fast as I could in a state of total terror and went to Mr Kempton's yard to ask for the dinghy. 'How did you get here?' he enquired in amazement, looking at my wet swimsuit.

'I swam.'

'Who told you to?'

'John Carberry.'

Mr Kempton was a decent man with daughters of his own. He got in the dinghy with me and rowed over to *Nguva*. As we arrived JC sauntered over and greeted him in his irritating pseudo-American accent. I'll never forget his look of astonishment as Kempton punched him full in the face and upbraided him for forcing his daughter to swim in such conditions. As on other occasions, when offered straight-up violence by another man, JC backed down and revealed that, like most bullies, he was a coward. For all his protestations over sporting prowess and daring he was not a very masculine man.

JC was a landlubber at heart and was extremely fussy that *Nguva* should always look spotless. One day, he, June, Maxwell Trench and I had been deep-sea fishing and caught a barracuda. They are fascinating-looking creatures with pointed faces and lots of teeth, including three the size of the eye-teeth on an Alsatian dog. When we landed it, Waiganjo was summoned to hit it on the head with a hammer

I was intrigued by these big teeth. Not aware that the nerves of a dead animal can continue to cause spasms I went up to it and felt the tooth. Suddenly the jaws snapped, biting through the tops of two of my fingers. It hurt like mad and it shocked me. I ran screaming through the saloon to Waiganjo who was always very kind to me and who saw to the wound. When I joined the others I was scolded severely for having dripped blood on the saloon carpet.

I was also inadvertently the cause for another upset. In the grounds of the Tudor House Hotel were frangipani trees, which I used to climb while the grown-ups were lazing around drinking or taking their nap. Geckos liked laying their eggs in holes in the frangipani and I used to collect these in a matchbox. I put the matchbox away in a corner of *Nguva* and forgot about it until one morning we arrived to find the boat crawling with baby geckos. No one knew how they got there.

JC's enjoyment of the luxurious *Nguva* was destined to be short-lived. When war broke out she was requisitioned for coastal defences by the British Navy. Then she was taken to Ceylon. I don't think he ever got her back — a fine irony for a man who detested Britain and hoped Hitler would win the war.

9

How I Finished with Finishing School

I had not 'fitted in' at the Ryrie school in Nanyuki and before long it was suggested leave. After the difficulties over hats and shoes i was decided that maybe it would be easier to educate me at home.

I was nine when Lisette came into my life Lisalotte Mack was the daughter of a cavalry officer in the Prussian army. She was extremely strict and particularly fussy about table manners. We still ate our meals separately from June and JC in the sun parlour. If I unthinkingly put my elbows on the table Lisette would creep up behind me, pick up my elbow and crack it down hard on the wood. The funny-bone is highly sensitive and it hurt like hell. But Lisette was one hundred per cent fair and she loved me. She fell in love with a local farmer and wanted to leave and get married, but JC wouldn't release her from her contract. 'You want to get married, take the brat with you,' he ordered. And she did Lisette married Selby Mumford, who had a coffee farm at Muringatu at Nyeri. Their house was one of the typical old settler homes built of hardwood and raised on stilts to discourage invasion by insects and other unwelcome creatures. The design may have defended the interior of the house, but the space underneath

124

which was cool and dry and sheltered, became a dusty haven for cats and dogs, and a maternity ward where all the unwanted puppies and kittens were born.

Lisette started married life with me at Selby's estate, sacrificing privacy perhaps more than they realised. One day we were down at the coast at Diani, where they had a house right on the beach. Because it was always so hot and humid here, the bedroom doors were like stable doors that you could look over. Intrigued by strange noises issuing from Lisette's bedroom one afternoon, I looked over the top of the door and observed, fascinated, human beings engaged in the act of copulation.

Lisette was a good rider and she tried to teach me. She had inherited the Prussian predilection for discipline and obedience from her officer father. I was frightened to go faster than a trot on Lelly and Lisette would expect me to canter. Instead of kicking Lelly on I would hold her back. 'Lelly won't canter,' I'd insist.

At this Lisette would bellow, 'Do what you're told!' and whack me and Lelly simultaneously. This would send Lelly off into a wild gallop, which would end up in a bucking spree. If she couldn't get me off that way Lelly would get down and roll. Then, when I was on the ground, she would spin round and throw both boots at me. There is a rule if you fall off a horse in Africa, where you may be out alone in the bush: hang on to the reins. This may mean you get dragged, but at least you'll be able to get home. Old habits die hard. In later years, when I was

125

water-skiing in Kingston Harbour, Jamaica, thi
vital lesson proved less than helpful. To m
friends' horror, instead of letting go when I fell,
held on and was dragged through the water, no
only half drowning in the process but, in thos
notoriously shark-infested waters, creating
come-and-get-me splashing, gasping bundle o
shark bait.

As long as Lisette was on the payroll, June anc
JC felt free to leave all matters regarding my car
to her. She may have been strict, but she believec
children should be handled with integrity anc
was prepared to stand up to her employers ove
it. On one occasion I had been invited to
Christmas party at the Nyeri Club. Lisette go
me ready, and June and JC were supposed tc
come back from wherever they were and take m
there. But they didn't. Lisette borrowed a ca
and drove me herself. When she met June and JC
in Nyeri she went for them, screaming abuse anc
yelling: 'You do not promise a child somethin,
and let it down.' I thought she was brave to sticl
up for me and it was nice to see them ticked of
so publicly.

JC could not keep Lisette indefinitely anc
besides, I was now eleven, the age when colonia
children were packed off to boarding-school
Most children attend two or three schools in th
course of their education. By the time I lef
school I had been to seven. The result of all thi
diversity is that my knowledge is uneven, to sa
the least. I know no English history, my grasp o
physics and maths is sketchy but I speak fluen
French and German.

There was no rhyme or reason in the way JC approached the question of my education. He clearly found the responsibility of parenthood burdensome. It would have been so much easier to do what most colonial parents did, which was to find an establishment that fitted the bill and simply leave me there. Instead, between the ages of eleven and fifteen I went to four different boarding-schools, one in England, one in South Africa and two in Switzerland.

What the various administrations headed by those dignified, God-fearing lady teachers made of John Carberry and his bizarre instructions one can only imagine. He made a point of writing to each new school and stipulating (i) that I bath every day, which was unheard of in boarding-schools of that era, and (ii) that I be excluded from all religious instruction. He sent me to a finishing school, where the next youngest pupil was sixteen, at the age of eleven. And to one school which wrote requesting permission to buy me new shoes as my old ones were outgrown (I had, after all, been there for a year without a break) he replied that girls with big feet were unattractive and that I should be made to continue wearing the old ones.

My first taste of the restrictive regime of boarding-school involved travelling 6000 miles to a place called Surrey in England. But I was going to have some ready-made Africa-raised company as two other girls from Kenya were bound for the same establishment.

Before we started at our new school we were to have an English seaside holiday. My

127

companions were the Stoyle sisters, Molly and Betty, who were a bit older than me, and their younger sister Peggy, who became my best friend. Their father worked for the railway in Nairobi and his wife had rented a house in the seaside town of Worthing in Sussex. June and JC joined them, though JC kept disappearing up to London. This was 1936 and Beryl Markham, the pioneering aviatrix and fellow Kenyan, was preparing her trail-blazing solo flight across the Atlantic. JC had offered to lend her the state-of-the-art plane he was having built for the trip and so was closely involved in her departure which was repeatedly delayed by bad weather. He lent the plane, a Vega Gull christened *The Messenger*, with its 3800-mile flying range, on condition that Beryl return it by the end of September as he wanted to take part in the pioneering Portsmouth — Johannesburg race. In the event, Beryl had to make an emergency landing in Nova Scotia, which damaged the plane, so he didn't get it back in time.

Like June Carberry, the Stoyles were great drinkers. They were drunk most of the time they were at the Worthing house. They didn't give a damn what we got up to as long as we didn't bother them. We took advantage of our freedom to become seasoned juvenile delinquents, breaking windows, stealing money and pinching chocolate from the local shops. Horses were our passion and we soon palled up with some boys who had a pony rank on the seafront. The boys, who were veteran street urchins, enjoyed encouraging these gently reared little girls into

128

mischief. They used to buy fish and chips, throw the chips on to the beach and then get us to fight for them. As usual, JC insisted I was dressed like a boy. Betty and Peggy wore dresses while I wore khaki shorts, but for working with the ponies my tomboy style of dress was more practical. Each day we used to go up to the stables where the ponies lived, get them ready and bring them down to the beach, then do the same thing in reverse when their working day was finished. The problem was that the stables were quite a long way from our house and I at least risked a beating if we were late for dinner. Roller skates had just come in and we decided to pinch a pair from a local shop. We concluded that it was less risky to nab one at a time, so we took it in turns. One day I acted the decoy, taking the shopkeeper away from the booty with some innocent request, while Peggy pinched one skate; a few days later Peggy played the decoy while I nabbed the other. We strapped on one skate each and used it like a scooter to zoom home in time for supper. Coming straight from the stables I always looked filthy and invariably got bawled at by JC.

He could never be around me for long without finding an excuse, however trivial, for a beating. He found his opportunity in the lavatory of the house in Worthing. It had an overhead cistern and a chain to flush it, the handle of which made marks on the wall when it swung. The marks were a hallmark of that type of flushing system and had built up over the years. Nevertheless I got blamed for it. I overheard JC say to June:

'I'm going away so you give her a bloody goo
hiding.' I vigorously protested my innocence. O
this occasion I was spared. Dorothy Stoyle, wh
never beat her children, came to my rescue
pointing out that it was her house and insisting
was not going to be beaten while she was i
charge. The holidays were great fun but all to
soon it was time to sample life at an Englis
boarding-school.

Greenacres School in Banstead, Surrey, wa
an English school, typically full of prohibition
where everything worth doing seemed forbidder
It was worst on Sundays when you were no
allowed to play any games or even listen to th
gramophone. All you could do was read th
Bible. To us freedom-loving Kenyan kids, used t
running wild in wide-open spaces, thes
restrictions were too much. Peggy and I lived fo
playing horses and on Sundays, the best time fo
playing as there were no lessons, we wer
forbidden. We made up our minds to sto
co-operating with the staff. When they asked u
anything we would reply only in Swahili. Th
headmistress was furious. She decided to starv
us into submission, telling us we would get n
food until we asked for it in English. At th
point Peggy cracked but I held firm. I have neve
been very interested in whether I eat or not an
besides, I was stealing food from the kitcher
When the end of term came we were requeste
not to return.

The experiment with English boarding-schoo
education having failed, JC's next idea was
Swiss finishing school. Lots of girls of my clas

ere sent to be finished in those days — but usually they had completed their secondary education beforehand. I was eleven when I was sent to my finishing school where all the lessons were conducted in French. What possessed JC to send a pre-pubertal child to a school of this nature I don't know. Perhaps the idea of my becoming fluent in French appealed to him. And why did the school accept me? The establishment was in Lausanne and was called Les Allières. The vast majority of the girls there were English, with a smattering of American and French. June came with me at the beginning of term. I remember being introduced to the big fat headmistress. She stroked my face and, to her consternation, I tried to bite her. This is what horses do if you stroke their faces and they don't like it. I was not used to having my face stroked and, at that age, receiving little in the way of social training from humans, I modelled my behaviour on horses.

The first thing they did at Les Allières was to teach me to write in the rounded script beloved by the French. Learning to write again and trying to understand maths and history in a foreign language was exhausting and dispiriting. I was deeply homesick there and felt the cold dreadfully. My room-mate was a sixteen-year-old French girl. She had been seduced by a much older man who had raped her and she used to terrify me with tales of what he did to her. She said he had a penis the thickness of a forearm and that it hurt. The only one I had seen like that was on my donkey and the thought that sex

might lead to injury worried me. I struggled i
an environment where everyone else wa
grown-up. I was so ashamed of not being as ol
as the others that I put red paint on my pants t
pretend I too had periods.

In the winter the school used to decamp to
chalet in Gstaad for winter sports. I hated skiing
In those days there were no ski-lifts and so yo
had to climb back up each time. Being so mucl
younger than all the others I got terribly tire
and cold. I also loathed sauerkraut, a dish w
seemed to be served every day for lunch. I
those days children were forced to eat everythin
on their plate. I used to whoosh my sauerkrau
into my napkin and then flush it down the loc
After my sunny golden Africa, Switzerlan
seemed a bleak, white, claustrophobic place an
I hated it. To try to cheer me up they arrange
for me to ride. The horse was called Lucifer.

But Les Allières did get one thing right.
didn't shine academically at my new school, bu
the staff were observant enough to see beyon
the obvious handicaps caused by being fou
years younger than everyone else and having t
cope with doing all your lessons in an unfamilia
foreign language. They found that I could no
see the blackboard and sent me for an eye test
which diagnosed myopia. Looking at the worl
through rose-coloured glasses may be a cliché
but when I got my first pair of specs my worl
did indeed look rosy. The improvement in m
academic performance and my personal happi
ness was dramatic. Alas, it was destined to b
short-lived.

At the end of my year in Les Allières I travelled to England, still savouring the novelty of a world in focus and proud to show off my new specs.

June met me off the train. As soon as she saw my glasses she shrieked: 'What the hell have you got on your face? Take them off.'

'But I can see . . . '

'I'm not going around with you looking like that!' And June took my glasses away.

Going back into the dark after that was terrible.

By the end of a year in Lausanne I was starting to speak good French, my writing had settled down and I had made friends. One day while we were staying with her mother I told June how I was looking forward to seeing a particular girl again.

I was stunned when she replied: 'You're not going back to Lausanne. You're going to a new school.'

The Institut Elfenau in Berne was another Swiss finishing school with certain similarities to Les Allières. There was no uniform, most of the girls were English and in the winter the school decamped to a chalet for intensive winter sports tuition. But there were significant differences. This time the lessons were all in German, a language entirely foreign to me. Having spent a year laboriously mastering the rounded script which is the hallmark of a French education, I now had to spend hours copying out letters on special double-lined writing paper so that I could acquire the

characteristic pointy up-and-down Germani
script. The obligation to write thus has lef
permanent scars. To this day, especially wher
capitals are concerned, I mix the two styles
writing a capital 'M' first in the French manne
and, two sentences later, in the German style.
was terribly handicapped by all these change
of direction. And, of course, I was still th
youngest child in the school by several years. T
try and compensate for this I was allowed to g
to the Tiergarten, an open-air animal park ir
the city, where there were ponies — Max
Micheli and Souci — which I used to ride.

In the winter, just as had happened at Le
Allières, the entire school moved up th
mountain for skiing, where the headmistress'
son Herman became our ski instructor. Ou
'Chalet Alpina' overlooked the village o
Grindlewald and had a splendid view of th
Eiger which, from that angle, seemed to b
turning towards us the craggy profile of a
human face. I continued to loathe skiing
which I associated with cold hands and tire
legs, but the Chalet Alpina overlooked a
skating rink, which brought much pleasure
That I did enjoy. Having become proficient or
my roller skates in Sussex, I was soon zooming
round the frozen roads of Grindlewald
annoying pedestrians. I tried figure skating and
was convinced I was destined to become a
new Sonja Henie, the ultra-glamorous
Norwegian figure-skating champion who was a
household name in the Thirties.

Although he never visited the Institut Elfenau

JC made his presence felt. He wrote to the school saying that I would not be coming home for the holidays but was to stay at school. This meant that some of the staff had to forgo their vacations in order to supervise me.

10

Seduced at Sea

At thirteen, and despite two years at finishing school, I was still very much a child. After all those years of envying the older girls, my periods had finally started but my body was still skinny and little-girlish. As for my thoughts, they were fixed firmly on ponies and dogs rather than on boys and romance. This did not please June who thought it was time I grew up.

She collected me from the Institut Elfenau in Berne and together we travelled by train through France to Antibes, where we were to spend the summer at the exclusive Hotel du Cap. Irritated by my lack of sophistication, June began her grooming lessons on the train. At lunch-time I requested my favourite drink — milk. I now know that you can never get milk in Latin countries, but then I thought everyone drank it. When none was forthcoming I asked for water. June wouldn't hear of it, saying that no one drank water in France because it gave you goitre. Everyone here, children included, drank wine and wine was what Juanita was going to have. Silencing my protests, she insisted I drank a glass of red wine, which to me tasted unbelievably acid and disgusting. The triumphant smile on June's face faded as the glass of wine reappeared abruptly — a projectile crimson continent on the

136

ocean of white damask. I was dragged from the dining-car with hideous threats ringing in my ears.

The Hotel du Cap, with its wonderful swimming pool surrounded by sun beds and huge wooded grounds full of pine trees which released their delicious spicy scent after dark, was rather smart and attracted a film star and show business clientele. June was in her element, working on her suntan at the poolside, buying clothes, sipping brightly coloured cocktails from giant glasses and cooing at men. Once she appeared with the country singer Burl Ives in tow. Unable to cope with the thought that Ives might think her old enough to have a thirteen-year-old daughter, June introduced me as her little sister.

While she was entertaining I was expected to keep out of the way and amuse myself. As usual, I was up hours before her in the morning. I loved the swimming pool where, thanks to tuition paid for by JC, I felt in my eel-like element. Not so the daughter of the film actress Marlene Dietrich who was a fellow guest that summer. Wrestling with teenage puppy fat, poor girl, in contrast to her svelte mama, she used to get up at dawn to take swimming lessons when she thought no one would see her.

Animals continued to appeal to me far more than humans and the hotel had a miniature donkey, which had been imported from Morocco. He was coloured like a Doberman — black all over with brown points. He was too small to ride so instead I used to take him for walks through the pine woods that formed the hotel's grounds. Off I set one afternoon like Red Riding Hood when, unbeknown to me, a wolf slipped in after me. A big burly chap I knew slightly as he was the attendant who put the sun beds out at the poolside came up beside me and suggested we sat down. Trustingly I complied. Seconds later he pushed me back against the ground and climbed on top of me. With one hand he pinned my arms to the ground while with the other he started to pull down my knickers. I was terrified. I fought like a wildcat and pleaded with him not to do it. I threatened to tell my stepmother. He laughed. 'You wouldn't dare.' In the end my screams discouraged him and he let me go. Of course, he was right. Whom could I have told? I certainly didn't take the donkey through the woods again.

I spent the rest of that summer swimming and going for walks, and trying not to think about what was going to happen in September. I was to go to yet another boarding-school, this time in South Africa. The only consolation was that the new school meant a sea voyage and I loved ships. As usual, it would be the German East Africa Line, its appeal undoubtedly heightened in the eyes of JC by its nationality. He instinctively sided with whatever country was most hostile to Great Britain and, as the situation in Europe deteriorated throughout the Thirties, his support for Germany became more strident. Most of our trips were from Kenya to Europe. This one was going to mean sailing through the straits of Gibraltar round the horn of Africa and down to

Cape Town. We travelled so often on these ships, which were all sister ships and therefore more or less identical, that I knew my way around. In these more democratic times there is only first class and tourist class. In the Thirties there was first, second and third class. The Carberrys, needless to say, always travelled first. The advantage of travelling first was that while we could go anywhere on the ship the other classes were not allowed into first-class accommodation.

June, in common with many men and women of that pre-air travel generation, regarded ships as a fertile source of casual love affairs. The warm tropical nights, the romantic moon shining on the sea, cocktails which flowed, the absence of witnesses combined to make these passenger ships of the Twenties and Thirties floating passion wagons. It goes without saying that children were expected to make themselves scarce. The shipping company played its part in lightening the burden of parenthood by providing children's dining-rooms. I was only too happy to leave June to her cruising.

We embarked from Marseilles in September 1938. This journey was to prove significantly different from previous ones. No sooner were we on board than the whole of Europe was placed on a war footing over the Czechoslovakia crisis. The captain of our ship, who was, of course, German, departed from his course and sailed west into the Atlantic to await orders from his government. Rumours that if the Allies declared war on Germany he would take the ship to Brazil precipitated a panic on board. I was probably the only passenger who hoped war would be declared and we would go to Brazil. I so detested the idea of another boarding-school.

To my intense disappointment the crisis was averted by Chamberlain's 'peace in our time' deal. Life on board resumed a semblance of normality. I was now old enough to leave the children's dining-room and join June at meal-times. Despite her signal failure to set an example in any other way, she remained as rigid as any Victorian nanny over my eating everything up. I noticed gooseberries and cream on the menu one day. Assuming the dish would be the sweet, juicy tropical Cape gooseberries you eat raw and which I adored, I enthusiastically ordered them. When I tasted the sourish, pippy, stewed green mess that was put in front of me I found it disgusting. 'They're not gooseberries,' I insisted, beholding English gooseberries for the first time.

'Yes they are,' replied June, in a voice which took me back to the incident of the crow years before. 'You ordered them. Now eat them.'

June's catch on this trip was Willy. He was one of the bar stewards so she was able to pursue her two favourite hobbies simultaneously without giving a second thought to what I might be up to. Willy had a colleague called Gustav who also worked in the bar. Gustav began to take an interest in me. Unlike the man at the Hotel du Cap who had tried to force me, Gustav was gentle and kind. When he suggested we slip into a vacant cabin — he knew just where to take me so that we wouldn't be disturbed — I agreed. It didn't take long. It hurt a bit and I knew from the red blood on the white sheets that I was no longer a virgin, but I can't pretend it was rape.

For a girl to have her first experience of consenting sex at thirteen and a half is pretty shocking today. In those days it was almost unheard-of. Why did I co-operate? In my defence I can only say that I was flattered by Gustav's attention — I was used to adults telling me to go away — and curious. As far as sex was concerned I was the original moral vacuum. JC had expressly forbidden any contact with religious teaching, which would inevitably have harped on the virtues of keeping oneself pure, and June made love the way other people shake hands. I didn't feel any shyness taking off my clothes in front of a stranger because I was used to nudity. June walked around naked at Seremai. The Trenches were similarly relaxed. The five bathroom doors were never locked. When you walked in there was often someone lying in the bath totally unconcerned. And the Africans bathed naked in the rivers. As for the sex act itself, I knew what to expect because I'd seen the mares and bitches at Seremai being covered. What I also knew was that if you have sex there is a risk of a baby. As soon as Gustav had disappeared I was overcome with panic. I didn't dare tell June as she would have beaten me and denounced Gustav. Instead, I confided in a Frenchwoman I had become friendly with. I told her we were in love to make it less shocking. She was pragmatic rather than censorious and lent me her douche, a widely used female contraceptive, which I had also seen hanging up in June's bathroom.

It was as we drew near Cape Town that I made a decision which was one day to affect my life dramatically. I decided that when I grew up I would live on a ship. That was how, over a decade later, I found myself one of a handful of women volunteering to serve in the Merchant Navy, a wonderful life I led for seventeen years. How I wished, as a reluctant soon-to-be pupil at yet another hated boarding-school, that war would break out. I absolutely didn't want to leave that ship.

War was not to be declared for another twelve months, however, and, with a leaden heart, I travelled up to Johannesburg on the train with June as planned. Roedean, my new school in the Parktown area of Johannesburg, was a sister establishment of the world-famous Sussex Roedean, ever a favourite with aristocratic families. It proved even worse than I had imagined. I was forced into a ghastly uniform of dark, scratchy gymslip, which we called a *djibba*, white shirt and horrible constricting tie which, try as I might, I could never work out how to knot. I, who didn't like wearing shoes, now found myself obliged to wear thick woolly stockings held up by suspenders sewn on to a Victorian-type cotton undergarment, which began at our shoulders and ended at the tops of our thighs. English friends at boarding-school at the same time remember a similar garment, though theirs was padded, which they called a liberty bodice.

The name illustrates English irony at its best.

Academically I was once again a disaster. True, I was back in my correct age group but, denied the glasses I needed, I couldn't see to do anything. Once again I came bottom in everything. I was accused of laziness, stupidity, not caring . . . I could speak French better than all the other girls, but I couldn't write it as I had never been taught any grammar. That was equally true of my grasp of German. The one light in the darkness was friendship. Hermione, who became my best friend in that intense, perfect way that only girls of thirteen understand, was the granddaughter of the then Earl of Moray. Her proper title was the Honourable Hermione Stuart and she grew up into a famous society beauty whose antics fascinated the gossip columns. Hermione didn't go to Roedean, but to St Andrews, which was another girls' boarding-school in Johannesburg, and we were drawn together by horses.

June Carberry had a boyfriend called Semmy Curlewis who had been a Kenya settler and was friendly with a man called Tommy Charles, who owned a stable of polo ponies which was next door to the school. I used to be allowed out on the occasional Sunday to watch polo at the Inanda polo club. Semmy also knew the Stuarts and it was through him that I met Hermione. She and I used to ride Tommy Charles's ponies. The stables were strictly out of bounds but I never got caught.

When holiday time came it was considered too far for me to go back to Kenya and an invitation

came for me to spend the holidays wit
Hermione. The Stuarts had a magnificen
50,000-acre cattle ranch in Bechuanaland calle
Saas Post. The nearest town was Mahalapy∈
Bechuanaland was arid semi-desert landscap∈
quite different from my temperate Whit
Highlands. Kipling's 'great grey green greas
Limpopo river, all set about with fever trees an
haunt of crocodiles' ran through their acres. An
there were crocs. Hermione and I used to thro∖
stones at them. At the Stuarts I discovered life a
it is lived in a normal, loving, rough-and-tumbl
family. Hermione who, even at thirteen wa
regal-looking, with luxuriant long fair hair an
slender gazelle-like limbs, had three brothers
Charles and James, who were twins, an
Douglas, who is the present Earl of Moray
Douglas was not into horses but rode a bicycl
with solid wheels, which I had never seen befor
and have not since. What did grow in that ari
soil was thorn and I suppose a pneumatic tyr
would have been ripped to shreds. Douglas wen
to Hilton College in Natal. This was a brothe
school of Wykeham, which I was to attend a yea
or two hence. Lord Doune, his father, had hi
own plane and landing-strip, like JC, and used t
fly him to and from school. Douglas was dee∣
into stamp collecting and didn't mix with us
great deal but the twins were little monsters i
the William Brown mould. The horses i
Bechuanaland all had hogged manes to discour
age tics and the trimmings from these frequen
short back and sides were very bristly. When
retired at night I would find, not just a∣

144

pple-pie bed, but one full of handfuls of these
vretched bristly clippings, which stuck to the
heets and were impossible to get out.

Saas Post, which was named after an Afrikaner
ho had a trading post there, was composed of
ast enclosures that went on for ever, in which
attle roamed. The manager was a big burly
Afrikaner called Fred Riggs. He had a horse
alled Sweep, which no one else could ride.
Iermione and I rode from after breakfast until
ark, although we weren't supposed to be out
fter dark. Her horse was called Gingernut, mine
vas an ex-polo pony called Roulette. We used to
et terribly hot and then we'd swim and bathe
ur horses in the river. Because of the crocodiles
ve were only allowed to swim if Fred Riggs came
oo. He would sit on the bank with his gun
ocked while we swam with the horses.

One day we went further than we realised.
Vater was scarce in that arid countryside and we
ound a dam, or pool in the river. It was full of
hirsty cattle standing around drinking. The
vater was less than crystal clear but we were
ying of thirst — we never thought to take any
rink with us — and we thought if it was okay
or cattle to drink it was fine for us. We gulped it
own, before suddenly realising how far we were
rom home and how late it was. On the way back
s darkness fell we were chased by a pack of wild
ogs. It was like being hunted by wolves and the
orses were as terrified as we were. The worst bit
vas the gates between the enclosures. You
ouldn't risk making a horse jump a wire fence
1 the dark and the gates were rather Heath

145

Robinson-like. We did get into trouble when w
got back, but we were so glad to be home that w
didn't object.

At the end of a day's riding Hermione and
would share a bath and soak in a solution c
Cooper's Dip. It was really an anti-tick treatmer
designed for livestock, but we thought it smelle
wonderful. It didn't protect me from the hazard
of riding in Bechuanaland, however. When
returned to school I developed swollen gland
and a raging fever. It was diagnosed as tick feve
and I was isolated to the san.

My friendship with Hermione was th
happiest relationship I had ever experienced. A
the end of our year together, as I was returnin
to Kenya, not knowing when we would see on
another again, we solemnly exchanged vests in
ritualistic celebration of *Bruderschaft*. I trea
sured the vest, its regulation red-printed Cash'
name tape bearing the legend H. Stuart, fc
many years. We kept in touch by letter throug
what for me were often bitter times and me
again after we were grown-up. I used to stay wit
her at Darnaway Castle, one of the two famil
seats at Forres, Morayshire. It was life in th
grand style, much as it must have been in JC'
young day at Castle Freke — all four-poste
beds, and intimidating maids unpacking you
suitcase and asking severely where your night
dress was. Hermione died far too young, killed i
a horrific accident caused by a speeding lorr
while out riding with her thirteen-year-ol
daughter. Saas Post was sold in the late Fiftie
when Hermione's father became Lord Moray. I

as broken up into five farms. Fred Riggs and is brother Theo bought two sections each. Fred iter 'went bush' and married a black woman, which was frowned on in those days. Theo, in a ouching display of loyalty to his Scottish-born master, named his portion of the ranch Darnaway.

I am, as I have said, a great believer in fate and regard fate as even-handed most of the time. Were the innocent, carefree holidays at Saas Post nd the happiness of finding a true friend ranted to me to bolster me up for what lay head? At the very least it had turned a year I ad been dreading into a cluster of golden memories. I was sad at parting from Hermione ut looking forward to rediscovering my beloved Kenya.

11

Spare the Rod and Spoil the Child

I returned to Seremai to find that there were t
be no more schools. Instead, as was often th
case among colonial families, a governess ha
been engaged to teach me.

I did not hate June Carberry. I did not eve
hate JC, though I was mortally afraid of him. Bu
I did come to hate Isabel Rutt. The Rutt was m
second — and final — governess. Lisett
Mumford had been strict, but fair an
fundamentally kind-hearted. The Rutt wa
vicious and manipulative. The Africans hated he
for the way she treated me and with characteris
tic perspicuity called her '*fitina*', which mean
'trouble-maker'. The fact that JC was profoundl
uncaring about my welfare gave her *cart
blanche* when it came to punishment and sh
laid about me physically with impunity. He
arrival made my life at Seremai increasingl
intolerable. She understood the mixture c
cowardice and cruelty that made up Carberry'
nature and delighted in acting as its channel. Sh
told tales, which got me into trouble, and the
gleefully administered the worst hidings I eve
endured.

I had returned from South Africa, apparently
with a South African accent. The Rutt woul
order me to read aloud, an ordeal at the best c

mes, in view of my sight problems and of what ʻas diagnosed years later as dyslexia. When, on ɔp of this, I mispronounced a word the Rutt ʻould lash me round the face till I became ʻightened to read. Years later, when I was staying 1 Ireland with my cousin Peter and his wife, I ʻas recalling my governess's viciousness.

'What was her name?' asked Joy, Peter's wife. ·y an extraordinary coincidence the Rutt had lso been Joy's governess — but had been sacked ɔr being too nasty.

Lessons with the Rutt took place in a strange uilding called the chalet which was some way ff from the main house. It had been installed ɔr some long-departed farm manager and was uilt on stilts. The downstairs was used as a store ɔr fruit. The schoolroom part was upstairs and very morning after breakfast the Rutt and I ʻould proceed to the chalet where she would 1ow me postcards of famous paintings and rder me to write essays on Leonardo da Vinci nd Botticelli's *Birth of Venus*.

To me the Rutt always appeared an ogre. To 1en, though not physically attractive, she was 1ore accommodating and they liked her. ʻhough June was Rutt's employer and might ave been expected to maintain a certain istance, they quickly discovered that they 1ared a taste for boozing and casual sex. This reated a sly complicity between them.

Yet even the most obnoxious of governesses annot poison everything. It was lovely to be ack at Nyeri; wonderful to see the houseboys nce more and the pets; great to savour the freedom of the open-air life and know that need never again wear a liberty bodice.

There was, now, to my chagrin, a certain respectful distance between the African *totos* and me. Before I went away they used to call me *nyawera*, or 'worker' because, unlike most colonial females, I was always busy, cleaning tack, grooming the horses or growing carrots in my own patch of the kitchen garden. Now I had become, to my regret, *memsahib kidogo*, or little mistress, to distinguish me from June who was *memsahib mkubwa*, or big mistress.

The Africans had nicknames for everyone. Apart from *fitina* for the Rutt, the most telling was the one they used for JC — *mcharicha*. This was the Kikuyu word for the long whip used on the teams of oxen, which acted as general beast of burden at Seremai, ploughing between the coffee plants and drawing carts laden with firewood, coffee or barrels of water. JC used to crack this whip at the Africans who worked on the coffee farm. It was, too, a pun as *mcharicha* also described JC's tall lean build. Nellie Trench was called *nyakanuria*, which translates as 'bottom-wagger'. She was rather tubby and when she got angry and wagged her finger the whole of her lower body wobbled. Maxwell was *bwana kabage*, which means 'boss-whose-ears-stick-out' and another coffee farmer called George Maxwell was known as a *bwana kisurya*, which means 'he who farts', for reasons one can only guess at.

Swimming had been the one competitive sport at which I excelled at Roedean and it was

150

wonderful to swim for pleasure again. At Nyeri the water in the flowing rivers was cool enough for trout and we often went off on trout-fishing parties with Lisette Mumford, my old governess, her husband Selby, and the Franks who ran a butcher's shop in Nyeri. Whenever anyone's line got snagged it was always 'the brat' who was volunteered to go over and untangle it. Swimming in the dams, which was what we called the fish pools made by damming the Chania river, was strictly forbidden, as they were infected with bilharzia. This is a serious tropical disease carried by snails which live in semi-stagnant water. There are two types, one which affects the liver and the other the bladder. Dan French and I never took any notice of this ban and swam to our heart's content. As the dam was full of tilapia fish, which are stickle-backed and painful to land on, Dan would expect me to dive in first to scatter them. When I refused he would pick me up and throw me in.

Another pleasure I rediscovered on my return to Nyeri was the taste of raw meat, an experience I look on as a gastronomic treat to this day. I was in charge of feeding the cheetahs and used to cut up the bucks we had specially shot outside the back door with the kitchen *toto*. From time to time, much to June's exasperation, I would pop a piece into my mouth. Of course I used to get worms. To try to teach me a lesson June used to worm me with the same tablets as she gave the dogs, Bob Martin's worm capsules, which resembled black olives. 'You eat bloody dog food,' she would say. 'You can bloody well be wormed like a dog.' And it worked.

Like most of the settlers who lived in Africa in those days I did not escape all the tropical diseases endemic in the continent. Apart from the worms that I contracted by eating raw meat I'd caught tick fever in Bechuanaland; malaria still continues to plague me today from time to time; and in the end my insouciance over swimming in the dam also caught up with me. When I was grown-up I began to suffer from terrible migraines and double vision. After a number of tests bilharzia was diagnosed. In those days the treatment was antimony, a potentially deadly poison. The idea was to administer a dose hefty enough to kill the parasite, but not quite sufficient to kill the patient. They gave it as an injection, handing you a bowl simultaneously to catch the vomit that this violent shock to the system inevitably produced. The poison did its work of turning me inside out — including producing a tapeworm several feet long which resembled a particularly disgusting dish of spaghetti — a legacy of years of pinching the cheetahs' supper.

A frequent visitor to Seremai was Beryl Markham, the aviatrix. She and John Carberry shared an obsession with flying and JC used to lend Beryl his mechanic, Monsieur Beaudet, whenever her plane needed servicing. Beryl was very tall, with blonde curly hair and, being a serious drinker with a tangled love life, she must have fitted effortlessly into the scene with the grown-ups at Seremai. In addition to being a fearless pilot, Beryl was also an experienced rider.

My pony Lelly had by now been replaced by okkie, a brown Somali pony. He came with the ame Jaribu, but in honour of all the South frican military personnel who had been drafted ito the neighbourhood because of the war I named him Springbok, which quickly became ortened to 'Bokkie'. Bokkie was an unbroken vo-and-a-half-year-old when I got him. I broke im myself and even though he was young and esh he was never horrible like Lelly. I paid 330 enyan shillings, or just over £15, for Bokkie, oney I had managed to raise by hoarding my ocket money and boosting it with tips I got om June who still paid me for plucking her yebrows, giving her manicures and soothing her ack till she fell asleep. Feeding Bokkie once I'd ot him was more of a problem as my pocket oney wasn't enough, so I used to steal from ine and JC. For once I was grateful for the eavy drinking that went on at Seremai. It meant iat no one was quite sure how much money iey'd had when they went to bed.

Riding in Africa was a much freer experience ian it is for children today. Because we rode on arth our ponies did not even need to wear oes. I never wore jodhpurs and a hard hat but ode in shorts, even if I did get the odd pinch om the stirrup leathers. I also rode barefoot, hich was possible because when I acquired okkie I was nosing around in the saddle room nd came upon a huge Western saddle. I don't now how it got there; perhaps JC had brought it ack from one of his many trips to America. The iddle was far too big for me but the stirrups

were like big boxes, closed at the front, int
which you put your feet. They were perfect an
meant that I could ride through the thornies
landscape without having to wear shoes.

I was very possessive of Bokkie and neve
allowed anyone else to ride him, a reaction mos
horsy people will understand. When Bery
Markham came to stay June used to make m
lend him to her. That was bad enough in itsel
but then Beryl would show off and do tricks
such as picking up a handkerchief from th
ground at full gallop. I would try them myse
after she had gone and invariably fall off. I hate
her for that.

★   ★   ★

Another of the nice things about coming hom
after such a long time away in Europe and Sout
Africa was rediscovering old friends such a
kindly shopkeepers and mildly eccentric loca
characters who had known me since I was
small child. One of these was the Chinaman.

Finding fashionable clothes was an endurin
problem for European women in Africa. It wa
the job of the Chinaman to try to fulfil this need
He would appear at Seremai at regular interval
— heralded by the barking of our dogs — ridin
a pushbike fitted with a carrier on which wer
piled a swaying tower of bolts of brightl
coloured cloth. He was always accompanied b
an African who was there to do the donkey work
He would spread his wares out on the verand
while June and the Rutt fingered and pondere

nd haggled. They always bought what the Chinaman called Americanee, which was unbleached calico, imported, presumably, from America. It was dirt cheap and very wide, and we used it for pillows and mattress covers. After the more refined dress material had been bought t would be taken into Nyeri, where an obliging nd skilful Goanese dressmaker would make it up according to the chosen pattern.

Nyeri town was small and unassuming, with the shabby, slightly desperate air of an old frontier town in the American Wild West. The main street was dominated by the Sandy Herd Store, a wooden building which you reached by climbing a short flight of steps. Sandy, who was the only European shopkeeper in the town, would sell you anything from a kitchen stove to a tin of Vim. Competing with Sandy were Mohamedalli Rattansi and the more modest Osman Allu, both of whom were Asians. In these emporia you could buy a plough or a pawpaw, a sack of *posho* (maize meal) or a baby's bottle. In addition to the bank and the post office, there was the Hygienic Butchery, run by Mr and Mrs Frank, who were German. We bought our delicious breakfast hams here and I used to enjoy helping n the shop, making sausages and washing tripe. The Franks were interned when war was declared.

Despite its modest size, the town boasted two hotels and a social club — all of which were used by June as watering holes — as well as a golf course. The fact that Nyeri prison was situated in the middle of it, so that golfers were aware of sad brown eyes observing them through barred

windows, did not seem to bother anyone. Thi
was Africa, after all.

The White Rhino Hotel was in the centre o
the town, respectable but provincial. Decidedl
more glamorous was the Outspan Hotel. Th
Outspan had a hairdressing salon where Jun
went to have her hair bleached and set. It ha
wonderful gardens when I was a child, includin
an aviary. The hotel was opened in 1928 and wa
owned by a man called Sherbrook Walker and h
wife Lady Bettie. Walker also built Treetops, th
smart safari guest-house in the Aberdare Fore
where Princess Elizabeth was staying when sh
learned of the death of her father, King Georg
VI. Children were not allowed in the bars s
when June met her friends I was left to amus
myself. I used to go and find the Williamse
daughters, Honor and Susan, to play wit
Alternatively, I would visit the stables in th
grounds where there were not just horses but
couple of zebras for guests to ride. Nyeri's mo
famous residents were Lord and Lady Baden
Powell who lived in a cottage called Paxtu whic
they had had built in the grounds of the Outspa
Hotel. She was a dear old lady who always wor
a floppy felt hat and went everywhere with a pe
hyrax tucked inside her shirt. A hyrax is a strang
animal which, though small, furry and somewh
catlike, is closely related to the elephant. Hyraxe
are nocturnal and emit blood-curdling shrieks
night. I don't know how they coped with that
Paxtu. We often used to bump into Lad
Baden-Powell carrying her hyrax, buying orange
or cooking oil in Osman Allu.

156

12

When the Lions Have Gone Hyenas Dance

(Kikuyu saying)

June's attitude towards me began to change after I came back from South Africa. She was still capable of bursts of disciplinarian zeal, which invariably ended in my being locked up without food or beaten, but she could see I was growing up. She began, subconsciously, perhaps, to see me less as the brat for whose safety she was responsible and more as a potential hunting partner. The grooming process began with my hair. She bleached my dark locks platinum to match hers and sent me to Theo Schoeten, the smartest hairdresser in Nairobi, to have it permed, which added five years to my appearance. In addition, she gave me a cigarette allocation. Every week I would receive fifty Players Cooltip cigarettes, which came in a flat pale-blue tin. I didn't smoke them all, but sold some to the Africans, which helped cover the cost of Bokkie's feed.

The Happy Valley set had never needed excuses for their convention-flouting behaviour. But nothing speeds up the sexual tempo of a community faster than a war. This was now 1940 and the war I had wished for on the German ship had been declared at last, though too late, alas, for me to be swept off to Brazil.

East Africa may have been a backwater in terms of bombs and shrapnel, light-years away from the nightly pounding of the Blitz and the rigours of rationing and clothing coupons, but there was the African empire to protect. A large part of Kenya's frontier bordered Italian Somaliland and Abyssinia, and geographically the colony was the heartland of Britain's Cape-to-Cairo dream. John Carberry, who went about bragging that Hitler would win, felt the effects of the war where it hurt most. Not only did the army sabotage his airstrip, but they also requisitioned his planes and his yacht and used them in the war effort.

JC was not bothered about appearing patriotic. He was shunned by many Kenya folk at this time for his outspoken pro-Hitler views talk that verged on treachery. I remember hearing grown-ups talk of violent arguments in the bar of the White Rhino Hotel in Nyeri and at the Outspan Hotel caused by JC proclaiming in his loud, brash way that Hitler was a far better leader than that old fuddy-duddy Winston Churchill, that he was a man of destiny and that he would be the victor. It was frowned on for people to go to the Eden Roc Club, which JC ran in Malindi, and at one stage Seremai was declared out of bounds to British troops although that could have been due to the fact that June, with her reputation as a drug user and heavy drinker, was regarded as socially undesirable. Nevertheless, mail to and from Serema was censored during the war years, which

158

uggests that there was suspicion over Carberry's ctivities. There has been speculation that JC was art of a Nazi cell that had been set up in Kenya ith the Earl of Erroll as its leader. It has been uggested that this cell was the skeleton of a olonial government-in-waiting should Germany in the war. I think it extremely unlikely that JC as ever part of anything so organisedly ubversive. The bullying aspects of Nazi ehaviour, the swaggering fascist hooligans, with eir kinship with the American gangsters he so dmired, were right up his street. But JC was too uch of an individualist to join a hierarchical rganisation. He got his kicks from scandalising ose around him.

While John Carberry preached Nazism June Carberry partied. The war gave her a heaven-nt opportunity to do what she liked doing best, hile appearing to be doing her patriotic duty. he held open house at Seremai for all forces ersonnel, British Army officers and South frican Air Force alike. June, with her gregarious ersonality, had been part of the Happy Valley et since her arrival in Kenya and on terms of lose friendship with fun-loving White Highland-rs like Jack Soames, Dot and Micky Lyons, alerie Ward, Pam Straughan and others. As a oung child I had been confined to the nursery ing and had never been introduced. Now that I as out of the schoolroom I began to be able to atch names with faces. Joss Erroll, who was to ake a dramatic intrusion into my life a few onths hence, used Seremai as a romantic ideaway in which to make love to Diana

159

Broughton, far from the eyes of her jealou
elderly husband, Jock Delves Broughton, but
never saw him.

The parties were highly informal. The guest
who included police officers from Nyeri polic
station, government officials and bank manager
dressed casually and helped themselves to a
endless stream of drinks from the bar. Whisk
John Collinses, brandy and soda, gin and toni
and pink gins were the order of the day, and n
one drank wine. There was dancing to the musi
of a wind-up gramophone, and guests came an
went constantly.

One of June's great friends was Valerie Ward,
good-looking blonde. Valerie, the daughter of
butcher in Nairobi, was socially quite humbl
but very pretty. She would come to parties an
stay overnight, but her husband Roddy Ward wa
rarely around. She, too, signed my autograp
book. She gave her favourite occupation a
dancing; her best subject as 'Me!!!'; her favourit
book as *Peter Rabbit*; her ambition on leavin
school to 'Go on the films'. As for what sh
feared most she wrote, enigmatically, 'Women
Valerie always brought her two Pekinese dog
with her. They used to be locked in her room a
Seremai. One evening I was told to feed them.
put the dishes down and as they were reluctar
to attack their food I picked up a tasty piece t
try to encourage them. One came up and bit m
I got scant sympathy from June when
complained. 'Serves you right. You never touc
animals when they're eating.'

The excesses of the Happy Valley lifestyl

160

idn't make for graceful ageing. I saw Valerie ears later in Nyali, Mombasa. She was still londe but her once pretty features were oarsened and lined. She had a glass in one hand nd a cigarette in the other. Between puffs on er cigarette, quite unselfconsciously, she took ulps from an asthma inhaler. It was a real)orian Gray experience.

Pam Straughan was another blonde, less lamorous than Valerie Ward, who was a regular t June's parties. She was one half of 'the wild 'ams' (the other was Pam Gaitskell), who were /ell known in Kenya for their high-spirited ·ehaviour. Their trademark was to dress in natching outfits, a favourite being black trousers nd red shirts topped with black, matching ombreros. They were often seen being driven ound the streets of Nairobi by assorted ·oyfriends, hanging on to the sides of 'box-body' ars. Box-bodies were the colonial equivalent of he pick-up truck and were associated with ransporting African workers and farm produce, ather than nicely brought up white girls.

There were flying enthusiasts, too. Sidney St Barbe, a regular guest, had his own plane. Our irstrip was a good mile from the house so air ·assengers needed collecting by car. St Barbe ised to buzz the house to let us know he was bout to land and needed transport sent down. Ie was later killed in a flying accident. Norman ˙urner, who was that rare bird, a colonial adult /ho liked children, was a regular guest. He used o fly up to Nyeri and I adored him. Other flying riends who used to drop in were the

Portuguese-born Chico Basto and his wife Lol
who had a farm at Naro Moru. We used to fly u
to see them at their farm because they had the
own landing strip.

The lady pilot Jane Wynne Eaton also came t
June's parties. Intensely patriotic, she put he
plane at the disposal of the war effort and ferrie
personnel and cargo all over the colony. Jane ha
a son called John who was slightly younger tha
me and whom I detested. I was expected to le
him play with my toys, which he always broke
One night I was told to go and put his light ou
— he was sleeping in one of the guest-room
— and found him playing with a gun. It was
beautiful little hand-gun, inlaid with silver an
mother-of-pearl, which belonged to his mother
Everyone slept with guns in those days as the
felt they never knew what might happen. H
raised the gun and aimed it at me. I shouted a
him to put it down, but he replied, 'It's all right
It's not loaded.' Hearing the commotion, th
Rutt came in. She, too, shouted at him to put th
gun down, carefully positioning herself behin
me as she did so. The boy kept insisting, 'But it'
not loaded.' To prove how stupid we were h
turned and looked at his reflection in the mirro
'See,' he shouted, pulling the trigger. The glas
shattered into a thousand pieces.

Often the parties were held at other people'
houses. Dot and Micky Lyons were grea
party-givers. Dot was the sister of the Hamilto
Gordon brothers, one of whom rode racehorse
at Nanyuki. They had a beautiful house a
Mweiga outside Nyeri, where they kept horses

Whenever I stayed there I used to ride a lovely grey mare called Ramona. Their house has since become the exclusive Aberdare Country Club from which the safari lodge, the Ark, a Treetops-style hotel, is run.

June embarked on love affairs so easily that sometimes at parties she would find herself double-booked. This was where she found a use for me. Usually I was expected to make myself scarce when June had company, but on this occasion at Seremai she invited me to join in the party. I was thrilled. For me it was a treat. June didn't give any particular reason why I was welcome but was not unhappy when a good-looking blond captain in the South African Air Force called Pieter took an interest in me. In his khaki bush uniform, with his forage cap pulled cheekily down over his right eye, his tanned face lit up by a heart-stopping grin, he looked like Apollo to me. I must have cut an incongruous figure at these anything-goes parties, still sipping my glass of milk, for I never developed a taste for alcohol. The pseudo-sophistication of my bleached hair and ubiquitous cigarette belied my baby face but these were troops who had been starved of female company for months. I doubt my new beau realised that his date was a year under the legal age of consent. He had been one of June's boyfriends but she was now launched on a new trail and had doubtless intimated that I was available. Pieter was stationed at Nanyuki which was not far from Mweiga, where Dot and Micky Lyons lived. June was very friendly with the

Lyonses and we often went up there to stay.
suggested to Pieter, who was nicknamed the
'golden wonder' because of his blond good
looks, that he come over when I was up there. We
rode out into the bush and there, miles away
from prying eyes, got off our horses and made
love.

The Rutt had been hired to look after me, but
as she and June became hunting partners the
Rutt began to be regarded less as a hired hand
and more as a social equal by party-givers. I
June and Rutty were going to a party I had to be
brought along too. When this happened the Rutt
and I, to my disgust, had to share a bedroom. Or
one occasion, Jack Soames entertained at his
farm in Nanyuki. On that night I was sent to bed
as the merry-making got under way, but I woke
up in the small hours to see my governess getting
into bed with a man in tow. From the grunts and
thumps that issued from the Rutt's bed it was
clear she assumed the brat to be fast asleep.
remember little of Jack Soames, who was very
much one of the Happy Valley set, beyond that
he ran a farm and had horses. James Fox, in
White Mischief, describes Soames as a sinister
pervert with a penchant for voyeurism. Apparently, he drilled holes in the ceilings of the
guest-rooms and peered through them to watch
the action. I wonder if Soames was spying on the
Rutt that night.

From time to time June and I would go to
Nairobi. June always stayed at the Muthaiga
Club and that meant dressing up. The Muthaiga
has become famous for hosting the extraordinary

inner between Joss Erroll and Jock Delves Broughton the night before Erroll was killed. In those days it was simply the smartest club in Nairobi, open only to Europeans and boasting a gentlemen-only bar, a cocktail bar, a restaurant, dance floor and its own golf course. Of particular interest to me was the fact that it also had dog kennels. Members were not allowed to bring dogs into the club and were expected to leave them in the kennels for the duration of their stay. The runs were full of Valerie Ward Pekineses and June Carberry Dachshunds. Usually, while June and JC stayed at the club, I would be dumped at my Uncle Gerald's house, which was about two miles away in Parklands, a residential district of Nairobi, where the houses were set in very big gardens. On one occasion, when I was about fifteen and in my blonde, curly incarnation, I stayed with June at Muthaiga. It was the early afternoon and most of the grown-ups were sleeping off their lunch, the way they do in the tropics, when an elderly Frenchman, whom I had sometimes seen with June, approached and suggested we went to see the dogs. We were just passing the curious sentry boxes that flanked the entry to the club when he grabbed my arm and bundled me into one of them. It was dark inside but not too dark to see what he was doing. In a trice he had exposed himself and was forcing my head down. I may have been sexually precocious but I was ignorant of the existence of oral sex. Struggling and revolted, I began to gag. I broke free and made a run for it, but I said nothing.

165

What did the Africans make of the way these
people, supposedly their masters, behaved? One
of the hallmarks of the lifestyle of the Happy
Valley set was exhibitionism, assisted by alcohol
and drugs. They all smooched in public. When
June or the Rutt had a boyfriend at Seremai they
would kiss and grope them, allowing themselves
to be fondled regardless of whether I or the
houseboys were present. They behaved as if the
Africans and I were invisible. It was a decadent
atmosphere. More than once I saw June grope
some man's crotch in the back of the car as I sat
in front with Gatimu and heard her squeal with
delight, 'Oh he's got a hard-on.' The notion that
women are entitled to sexual pleasure, indeed
the whole idea of romantic love between men
and women, was alien to African culture. For
one thing, African women in those days were
usually circumcised, so that they did not
experience pleasure in sex. This was a society
which sold daughters and bought wives. You
never saw Africans cuddling and kissing publicly.
It was one thing for men to screw around, but
the wife risked a beating if she was unfaithful
because she had been bought. What the Africans
thought when they saw how my stepmother and
my governess behaved when JC was away, how
they retained any respect for Europeans, I can't
imagine.

13

Early Love

In the midst of the African sunshine Isabel Rutt was my Snow Queen, bent on turning my life to ice. Thanks to her I was constantly in trouble during this period of my life, beaten for trumped-up misdemeanours, locked in my room on the most trivial pretext, calculatedly isolated from those who would have helped me. I was not alone in hating the Rutt. She treated the houseboys with arrogant disdain, as if she were the *memsahib* herself and not just a hired hand. She was forever criticising me for fraternising with them and tried hard to prevent my visits to the kitchen, where I would infuriate her by chatting to Kimani, the cook, in Swahili, which she didn't understand.

One day, when June was away on a shopping trip to Hong Kong, the Rutt decided to take me to Nairobi. Although she didn't know how to drive, on the way back she decided she would have a go and made Gatimu, who always drove, sit in the back. About halfway between Nairobi and Nyeri she lost control and the car ploughed into a bridge. The impact threw Gatimu forward, causing him to hit his Adam's apple on the back of the front seat. The poor man was in agony and couldn't speak. But the Rutt was so shaken by the accident that she insisted Gatimu get in the front and take over the driving again.

During this time the Trenches were more of a lifeline than ever. I stayed with Nellie while June was away in the Far East, helping in the dairy and generally looking after the animals. Nellie had a donkey which, because of his long ears, was called Sungura (which means rabbit in Swahili). Sungura was in foal and to my delight when the foal was born Nellie gave him to me as a birthday present. A baby donkey is the most enchanting animal imaginable. This one had a black moustache and I called him Hitler. Hitler, my baby donkey, lived in the same stable as Bokkie and when I rode out on Bokkie Hitler used to follow us.

It was the Rutt who engineered the ban on my visiting the Trenches. To June she suggested that they might be getting to hear more than they should about what went on at the parties. To JC she whispered that the Trenches might criticise his right to discipline me as he saw fit. Her words fell on fertile ground. The business side of the partnership was starting to show signs of strain, with Maxwell increasingly resenting the fact that Carberry led a playboy lifestyle while he did all the work. For me the ban was a catastrophe. I loved Maxwell and Nellie Trench who always behaved protectively towards me and whose hard-working, decent household provided an attractive contrast to the drunken, strident atmosphere which prevailed in the Carberry ménage.

The Africans liked the Trenches too and the boys devised a system of look-outs to help me circumvent the ban, though I could never again go to them spontaneously for help in a crisis. I continued to go round early in the mornings to help in the dairy before the Carberrys had woken up. I used to ride round on Bokkie, taking a back route through the coffee so I couldn't be seen from the house. I would tie Bokkie up at the back of the Trenches' house and two *totos* would mount guard, one near the Trench house, the other beside the petrol pumps near the stables between the two houses. If the Rutt appeared the first *toto* would utter a high-pitched sharp 'ku'. The other *toto* would acknowledge this with an equally high-pitched 'ma' and run to warn me. I would leap on Bokkie and gallop off.

When fate intervenes in our lives it often does so with no warning. It is only when you look back that you see that that was the day which changed your life for ever. I had no inkling, when I got up that morning that anything unusual was going to happen. The Rutt, as I have said, was always on the look-out for reasons to punish me. She had discovered that, though he was never prepared to whip me himself, John Carberry liked to watch, so she was at her most creative when he was at Seremai. Since the Rutt's arrival June had begun to insist, in a new form of bullying, that any letter I sent or received had to be read by her. It was yet another way of isolating me and preventing me from 'telling tales'.

On this particular day I received a letter from a girl called Hilda who lived in Nairobi. Holding out her hand June commanded, 'Give me the letter.'

I have always had a highly developed sense of justice. It seemed so unwarranted an intrusion into my privacy — and by people whose moral authority was deeply questionable — that I decided to stand firm. 'No. I won't.'

'Give me the bloody letter,' bellowed June.

'No. You've always told me it's wrong to read other people's letters.'

At this, June, outraged at being thwarted, lunged at the letter. As she did so I decided I would sooner miss reading it myself than give it to her. I tossed it on to the fire.

All hell broke loose. The incident was reported to JC. He ordered that I should receive a beating for the double offence of disobedience and defiance. The beating was not to take place at once for JC liked to turn the screw by telling me that I would be beaten but not specifying when, to give me time to sweat. When the time came JC issued detailed instructions. I was to pull down my pants and lie across one of the armchairs with both my hands touching the floor. With JC looking on the Rutt took the rhino-hide whip and gave me twelve strokes, more than I had ever had before. It was excruciating. My back and bottom were a mass of blood, with angry welts which remained for days. 'Beat her until she screams,' I heard JC say. I remember thinking, 'I won't scream — just to spite him,' but I did. For most of my life I have kept a diary. The note for 17 June 1940 reads simply: 'Hilda wrote. Hell to pay for me.'

Even the most submissive dog booted or cuffed once too often will decide enough is enough. That day I made up my mind to get out, whatever the consequences. I knew if I stayed I would end up like them and I was determined not to. I realised I would have to be patient. I was in the middle of Africa. I was a minor and the daughter of a prominent settler. In those days the authorities did not believe in intervening in a parent's methods of disciplining his child. If I had set off down the road with my suitcase I would have been brought back and whipped again.

What I did do, a few days later, was go to the police. My plan was to leave Seremai as soon as the opportunity presented itself, but I was concerned that JC would try and get me back. I thought that if a description of the injuries the Rutt and JC had inflicted on me were placed on record at the police station then JC would not be allowed to have me back. I decided to go down the factory road and take the short cut to Nyeri, which knocked a couple of miles off the journey. It hurt getting on Bokkie but I managed. The policeman in charge was a young European. I pulled down my pants and insisted he look at my bottom and write what he saw in the observation book. The poor chap was very embarrassed.

Five days after the beating John Carberry told me that just for good measure he was going to sell Bokkie, the pony I had spent such a long time breaking and taming. He put posters advertising him up in Nyeri town, but JC wasn't popular and everyone knew Bokkie was my pony. Nobody applied to buy him and the posters were torn down.

Life resumed a sort of normality. I was increasingly left alone with the Rutt while June pursued an active social life in Nairobi. When June and JC were away and I was on my own with the hated Rutt I would sleep, not in my usual room at the nursery end of the house where the windows had wire mesh across them but in one of the bedrooms close to the drawing-room which looked out on to the veranda. One of the legacies of an African childhood is that I am not afraid of much in the natural world. But I am afraid of leopards. Even when I see one in a zoo and our eyes meet I can feel the hairs on the back of my neck prickle. It is a well-founded terror. The leopard is a dangerous, unpredictable animal who, unlike most of the other cats, is not afraid of man. Leopards roamed the White Highlands in fairly substantial numbers. I would often lie awake in bed in the pitch dark and imagine that a leopard was crouched outside, waiting to spring in through my window. I was not allowed to have a light on, even though I was always frightened of the dark and I was obliged to leave my window open because the adults deemed fresh air to be healthy. This may seem odd, in view of the presence of leopards, but though leopards had been known to take dogs off the veranda it was unusual for them to come into a house.

That night, as I lay in bed, I heard a rustling on the veranda. At first I thought it was one of the houseboys and that what I had heard was the whooshing made by a *kanzu*. I switched on my light and looked out of the window, my heart

172

thudding. Crouched under the ping-pong table immediately outside, ready to spring, was the embodiment of all my terrors. The leopard's eyes reflected the light in my bedroom like the fluorescent green hands of a luminous clock. His gaze held me and paralysed me. Leopards do this. I have seen one walk up to an antelope and kill it without encountering any resistance. I stood mesmerised, looking into its lit-up eyes. Then suddenly I snapped to. I gave a blood-curdling scream and rushed out of my bedroom door into the passageway. Still screaming my head off, I headed for the Rutt who was sleeping in June's bedroom. As I ran I tried to slam the door behind me but, as happens in nightmares, I didn't have any shove and it didn't shut. As I hammered in panic on the door of my stepmother's room I knew the leopard must be close behind me and turned, sobbing, to face it. But it wasn't the leopard. It was Gatimu who, hearing my screams, had thought the Rutt was beating me and had rushed in from the courtyard to protect me. I gasped out 'Chui! Chui!' which means leopard in Swahili. Gatimu ran off into the dining-room, took out a gun from the cupboard and went after the leopard, which by now was running away across the lawn. It was a close call. The next morning we found claw marks where it had sprung up at the window.

Not long after this I had my first proposal of marriage. One night a young British Army officer decided to take advantage of June's well-known open-house hospitality. He was stationed at

173

Kiganjo, just outside Nyeri, where the British were engaged in building a British military hospital, and was probably in the Royal Engineers as he wore an engineers badge on his uniform. His mother ran a nursing home in Nairobi and he had grown up in Africa. His name, I believe, was Alastair Scott but I knew him as Scottie. I doubt that he was much older than I was. He was certainly not put off by the fact that at June's parties I preferred milk to gin and tonic and he seemed quite taken with me. A note in my diary for 16 August 1940 reads: 'First time Scottie liked me.' Just turned fifteen, neither child nor woman, I was terribly lonely at Seremai. What's more, I was used to being reviled by the adults I knew. My feelings for Scottie grew stronger and on 29 August I wrote in my diary — in Swahili so that the long-nosed Rutt wouldn't understand if she found it — 'First time Scottie slept with me.'

Scottie used to drive over from his base at Kiganjo, park round the back of the house near the cheetahs' run and climb in through my bathroom window. I was not sexually awakened at this stage in my life but I was receptive to Scottie's love-making in the way the bitches and mares I had seen all my life were receptive to their males when the time was right. I had received no moral guidance from the adults responsible for me. No one had spoken to me about the perils of predatory males or the need to keep myself pure for my future husband. My stepmother committed adultery as readily as she downed a whisky and the only moral lesson to be

174

earned from my governess was that a party constituted foreplay. Scottie was an affectionate and kindly lover and I, starved of the family kisses and cuddles most children take for granted, relished his affection. Scottie became quite serious. The diary entry for 29 September 1940 reads, 'Scottie asked me to marry him. He gave me his watch. Rutty took it away.'

This was typical of the Rutt's particular brand of nastiness. She had watched me falling in love. I never knew when I was going to see Scottie again and when the watch, my only link with him, went I was terribly upset. Scottie's nightly visits must have been spotted by the Rutt because one night she and June tore themselves away from their own pleasures to lay a trap. The Rutt lay in wait for Scottie with a loaded pistol. The idea was to give him a fright rather than do any actual damage. I woke up to hear a gun being fired. I understood about guns and I knew that when a bullet hits something you hear a dull thud. That's what we heard. The Rutt was in a state of total panic, thinking she'd shot Scottie. What she'd hit turned out to be the soil pipe of the lavatory next to my bedroom. Scottie fled. The entry in my diary for 12 November 1940 reads: 'Scottie at window. He was nearly shot with a gun. Locked in room.' From then on my door was fitted with a staple and hasp which was secured with a large padlock. Every night when I got into bed the Rutt would padlock me in. According to my diary this was not relaxed until February of the following year when, I suspect, June and JC were expecting a visit from police investigating the Erroll murder. Being locked in was a punishment I incurred more and more frequently during the Rutt era. Sometimes I was incarcerated during the day without regular meals and, because it was rather isolated from the rest of the house, the windows in my bedroom were fitted with expanded metal mesh so there was no escape. But for the courage and kindness of the houseboys, who knew the Rutt's game, it would have been even worse than it was. I was fond of Kimani, the elderly cook, who had always been kind. Now he showed he was brave too. I would hear a little tap on the mesh and a voice calling softly, 'Memsahib kidogo, I've brought you some food.' And delicious it would be, not solid English stuff such as we ate in the dining-room, but the sort of food I've always preferred — a sweet potato, an oiled maize cob, a piece of fruit.

The Rutt saw that Scottie made me happy and determined to break up our romance. My diary entry for 18 November states, 'Scottie under bluff arrest by police.' I imagine the authorities had been told I was under age. I never saw him again.

Towards the end of January that year Lord Baden-Powell died. He had originally planned to retire to South Africa but he had been so taken with Nyeri, as he paused there on his way south, that he had stayed. For years he had lived with his wife in the cottage in the grounds of the Outspan Hotel. The founder of scouting was our most illustrious resident and his funeral was a grand affair. The South African artillery provided

176

the guns and the Kings African Rifles the band. He was laid to rest in Nyeri's small hilltop cemetery at the foot of which flows the same Chania river that powered the coffee factory at Seremai. I took my small box camera along to record the event. Later a headstone was erected at the grave inscribed with a circle with a dot in the centre, the scouting symbol for 'gone home'. I photographed that too.

The following day an African peddled up to Seremai with a telegram.

I was about to become involved in one of the century's most fascinating murder mysteries.

14

The Erroll Murder

The telegram, which arrived on 26 Januar
1941, was from June Carberry. The Rutt and
were alone at Seremai. June was in Nairob
staying, as I was to discover later, with a
Englishman called Sir Delves Broughton and hi
new wife Diana. Clearly something dramatic ha
happened. As soon as she had read the telegran
the Rutt called Gatimu and told him to get th
car ready. We were going to Nairobi. This was
journey of a hundred miles along bumpy, dust
roads and meant between three and four hour
in the car. As we drove the Rutt tersely sketche
in all she deemed the brat needed to knov
— that Lord Erroll had been shot in the sma
hours of the previous morning — and that th
police were hunting his murderer.

Josslyn Victor Hay, Earl of Erroll was
Scottish aristocrat with a Casanova lifestyle an
a heart-throb reputation. He arrived in Kenya i
1923 in scandalous circumstances, having elope
with Lady Idina Gordon who had already bee
married twice. Lady Idina's house parties a
Clouds, her home in the White Highlands, wer
famous for sex. Elaborate rituals were devised t
encourage couples, many of whom belonged t
the minor British aristocracy, to swap partners i
an atmosphere heightened by alcohol and drugs

It was to describe the bohemian lifestyle of Lady Idina and her friends, who lived around the valley of the Wanjohe river in the Aberdare mountains, that the name Happy Valley was coined, and to their games that the expression 'Are you married or do you live in Kenya?' referred.

In the early hours of 24 January 1941 Lord Erroll's car was found in a ditch. Inside was the body of the philandering Earl, his head pierced by a single bullet fired from close range. Erroll's love life was a tangle of vanquished — and abandoned — wives and irate husbands. Any number of men or women could have pulled the trigger. Suspicion immediately fell on newly arrived settler Sir Jock Delves Broughton, with whose new wife, Diana, Erroll was conducting a very public affair.

I had heard of Lord Erroll, but never met him. Since I didn't know either Sir Delves or his new wife I had no inkling as to the motive and therefore no ideas as to who might have committed the crime. As we drove I thought ruefully of how I would rather be riding my pony than heading for a tedious day spent among adults whose drinking and trivial chit-chat bored me. We drove straight to the house the Broughtons were renting. This was at Karen, a residential district of Nairobi, named after Karen Blixen, the *Out of Africa* author. The land had originally been part of Blixen's coffee farm, which was one of the first in East Africa. It was a fairly average European-style house, two storeys high, built of quarried stone and roofed, as were

179

most of the houses in Nairobi, in Mangalore tiles imported from India. It had a large garden and — a feature I always checked for — stables. June came out as we arrived and introduced us to Sir Delves Broughton, whom she addressed as Jock. He was a tall man, elderly to my young eyes, but able-bodied. The four of us went in to lunch, with no sign of Diana Broughton.

The atmosphere was strained in the extreme, with much scraping of knives and forks, and spasmodic, stilted conversation. Halfway through the meal the door opened and a young woman came in. Much has been written of Diana's haughty beauty, her perfectionist elegance and hunger for expensive jewellery, diamonds and pearls for preference. That was the image she presented to the world as she grew into her role of doyenne of Kenya society. But on that day she had been in Africa less than two months. It is ironic that I, a teenage girl who only saw her twice, should have glimpsed, on each occasion, a face she never showed to anyone outside a small circle of intimates. What I saw was a young woman with reddened, swollen eyes, no make-up and dishevelled hair. She sat at the table, waving away all food and sobbing quietly, while the others wrestled with the embarrassment created by this very un-English scene. At the end of lunch June announced that she would drive Diana, who was still weeping, back to Nyeri to try to distract her. The Rutt and I were to follow with Gatimu in our car.

Alone among all of them Jock Broughton was conscious that the lunch had been a bizarre xperience for a child of my age. Just as I was reparing to leave he enquired if I liked horses. eeing my face light up he asked if I would like o see the stables. Children can be callous and or me, cooped up with a crowd of adults bsorbed in a problem I didn't understand, the ccasion had been pretty tedious. This was an nexpected treat.

Sir Delves led the way to the stables, which ere at the back of the house. At his subsequent ial for murder, much was made by his counsel Iarry Morris of his having a limp which, it was laimed, would have made it impossible for him o walk the two miles back from the murder cene to the Karen house. The limp was pparently contracted in mysterious circum- ances connected with Broughton's being nvalided out of the 1914–18 war. I didn't notice limp. What I did notice, as we approached the ables, was the muck heap, which was nouldering. This was not unusual. In that limate spontaneous combustion was an every- ay fact of life. During the rains delicious ushrooms grew on people's muck heaps but hat was odd was that on top of this one, lready partly consumed by the fire, was a pair of *ikkis*, or trainers. No one who lived in Africa estroyed old or outgrown clothing. You passed on to the servants. It didn't occur to me that ere was a sinister reason for the *takkis* being ere. I was simply shocked at the waste. I asked ir Delves why he hadn't given them to one of is servants. He looked surprised but didn't ally have an answer.

181

After admiring the horses, one grey, one a ba
I left with the Rutt and Gatimu for Nyeri. Jun
and Diana had already gone and Sir Delve
remained on his own. He looked forlorn as w
drove away and I felt sorry for him.

Questioning the Rutt during more than si
hours spent bumping along in a car that day,
managed to piece together the outlines of th
drama. The reason Diana was so upset wa
that, although she had only married Sir Delve
in November, for weeks she had been having
passionate affair with Lord Erroll. I had ofte
heard the silk-suited, bow-tied, hard-drinking
wife-swapping Erroll talked about at Serema
as all the women like June Carberry found hir
very attractive and would love to have slep
with him.

June had realised that she was likely to be
key witness in any murder trial and, as JC wa
away in South Africa at the time, had summone
us for moral support. Even I could see that sh
was an important player. She was one of the las
people to see Erroll alive and had gone hom
with the man who was the most obvious murde
suspect. She was staying with Jock and Diana o
the night of the murder and had spent the firs
part of the evening with all three of them at th
Muthaiga Club. Much was made at the trial c
the unconventional dinner quartet, at which Jun
had partnered Jock, and Diana, his wife c
weeks, had behaved as if she was with Errol
After dinner Erroll had taken Diana dancing a
Claremont Road House, another club outsid
Nairobi, having agreed, in a convoluted nod a

182

onvention, to Sir Delves's request that she be
ack by 3 a.m.

We arrived back at Seremai after June and
Diana. Diana had already retired in the
uest-room, which led off the sitting-room. June
vas in a state of high excitement over a
ollection of Arab knives, or *jambias*, she had on
ier mantelpiece, saying we ought to put them
way. She thought Diana was suicidal and was
rightened that she might use one of these to kill
ierself. At one stage of the evening I was told to
ake something in to Diana. The sight that
reeted me was extraordinary: she was lying on
he wonderful wooden bed in a state of deep
listress with mementoes of Joss Erroll scattered
ll over her body. She was clutching his army
orage cap and sobbing. All around her Erroll's
eatures stared out of dozens of black-and-white
ihotographs.

Diana was still distraught the next morning
nd June decided to take her up to Jack
ioames's farm at Nanyuki. There was always a
iarty atmosphere at this place, with its
vonderful grounds, and June hoped it would
heer Diana up. The Rutt went with them and I
vas left alone at Seremai.

At some time in the afternoon I heard the
logs bark and, to my surprise, saw that it was
ock Broughton. He had clearly hoped to find
Diana.

'Where is everybody?'

'They've gone to Nanyuki.'

'Diana too?'

'Yes.'

He had driven a hundred miles along hilly and winding roads, which reduced one's speed to thirty miles an hour. He was weary and seemed disappointed and upset. I didn't quite know what to do with an elderly man in an emotional state so I called for one of the boys and asked him to bring us tea. I warmed to Jock Broughton. He had been thoughtful towards me the day before at the strained lunch in Karen, taking me to see his horses, and I hated the behaviour of the people in the Happy Valley set. They were always drunk and loud, forever going off with other people's wives, continually screaming abuse at some African. Amid this raucous, frantic lifestyle Broughton seemed an outsider. As the conversation faltered I hit on an idea. I would ask him to sign my autograph book. Broughton happily complied with my request. He revealed that his favourite animals were horses and bears. When he came to the question 'what do you fear most?' he hesitated before writing 'loneliness'. I still have my autograph book. It was a poignant admission by a man already rejected by his bride of a few weeks. Then he signed his name and the date, 27 January 1941.

After tea I decided to return the favour of the day before by offering to show Broughton my pony Bokkie. As we walked round to the stables he opened what was to be the most extraordinary conversation I have had in my life.

'I don't want you to be afraid but the police are following me.'

'Whatever for?'

'They think I killed Joss.'

'Oh, how ridiculous.'

There was a pause. 'Well, actually, I did.'

I wasn't shocked. I was intrigued. 'How?'

Broughton then told me that while Joss was in he house saying good night to Diana he climbed nto the back of Erroll's car. When the vehicle lowed down at the junction of the Karen and Ngong roads he shot him.

I was fascinated — and deeply flattered. In choolgirl circles there was always a code of ilence attached to secrets, but this was far and way the biggest secret anyone had ever confided o me. 'I'll never tell anyone — even if they orture me,' I said.

Broughton evidently believed me. He gave a ittle laugh. 'Do you know, the police watched ne dispose of the weapon.'

He explained that on the way up to Nyeri he had stopped at Thika, where the Chania river blunges down in a spectacular waterfall. He had barked, walked over to it and dropped the gun nto the water. The police were parked some way off — too far, he thought, to have seen.

At this point we heard the sound of a car outside. It was June and the Rutt bringing Diana back from Nanyuki. As soon as she saw Broughton Diana flew at him like a wildcat, bunching and clawing at him, and screaming that he had killed Erroll. It was awful. Like most hildren, I loathed rows and I fled.

I never saw Broughton again.

People may find it hard to believe that a man n his sixties would confess to a child he hardly

185

knew that he had killed his wife's lover. We were after all, living in an era when a conviction for murder meant the rope. I don't find it so hard to understand. Perhaps in me, a child, Broughton sensed a fellow outsider. The lunch at Karen had been emotional and strained in the extreme. June had then taken Diana off, leaving Broughton alone with time to contemplate his wife's total lack of feeling for him. He, on the other hand, was deeply in love with her and had set off, doubtless not knowing how arduous the journey would be, to be with her. When he arrived at Nyeri, physically and emotionally at a very low ebb, there was no one there but a young girl and his secret blew out of him.

Two weeks later, on 17 February, a policeman called Inspector Gribble called at Seremai to question me, having discovered that I had spent time alone with Broughton. Before he came June Carberry drilled it into me that I must not say anything that would get Jock into trouble because if I did he would swing. Her warning made a deep impression on me. Until then I hadn't grasped the full import of my secret — that I held Jock's life in my hands. But June needn't have worried. I was not going to give away anything that would incriminate Jock. In my eyes he was the good guy. I sympathised with his hostility to Erroll and could imagine how painful and humiliating the very public affair with Diana must have been. Over the years, to save my skin, I had become an accomplished liar. Obstructing adults was something that came naturally and when Gribble began his questions

I played the dense, uncomprehending child.

The police decided that I was an unreliable witness. They must have had a trying time of it. Convinced that Broughton was their man, they encountered a wall of silence, obstruction — even ridicule — from the settler community who closed ranks against them as they tried to piece together the clues.

June and Diana altered their attitude dramatically once it became clear Broughton would be charged with murder. June had encouraged the affair between Diana and Erroll, to the point of lending them Seremai as a love nest. Yet at the trial her evidence — that Broughton was too drunk that night to have left the house, shot Erroll and then walked two miles back from the murder spot — played a crucial role in his acquittal. Diana, who must have felt a certain amount of guilt at the mortal danger Jock now found himself in, was responsible for flying to South Africa and hiring the redoubtable — reputedly infallible — barrister Harry Morris. Morris asked for the moon and got it. His fee was £5000 plus expenses, topped up by a bottle of whisky a day. He also signed my autograph book. His name is there, dated 4 June 1941.

The settlers were less than helpful in guiding the police to their man. The murder inquiry was led by Superintendent Arthur Poppy, head of the Nairobi CID. While his subordinates were considered adequate to question a child, when it came to interviewing Erroll's former wife, the Queen of Happy Valley Lady Idina, nothing less than Poppy would do. He went up to Clouds,

Lady Idina's house in the Aberdare mountains
On arrival he shouted the traditional 'hodi?
('may I come in?"), upon which a Somali servan
appeared. When Poppy asked if Lady Idina wa
available the servant motioned him to take a sea
on the veranda and disappeared into the house
A few moments later the veranda door opened
again and Lady Idina appeared. She was wearing
high-heeled shoes and smoking a cigarette in
long-necked holder. Apart from that she wa
stark naked. She calmly sat down on a sofa
looked him unblinkingly in the eye and said
'Well, Sergeant Poppy, can I help you?' Poppy
told a senior colleague in the Nairobi police tha
it was the most difficult interview he had
conducted in his entire service as a policeman.

Jock Delves Broughton went on trial fo
murder on 26 May 1941. They planned to cal
me as a witness for the defence, so I can
have said anything damaging to the police. To
familiarise me with the procedure in a murder
trial I was taken to the courthouse at Nyer
where a young Kikuyu woman was on trial for
having killed her baby. That trial affected me
for years to come. I had been brought up in
very anti-British household. We colonials didn'
relish being told what to do from 6000 mile
away. As far as we were concerned the British
were BLIBs, which stood for Bloody Lousy
Imperial Bastards. I was very upset at what
saw as the appalling injustice being meted ou
to this African woman in a circus which called
itself a British law court. Sixty years later I am
still appalled. The woman had killed her child

because it had leprosy. In killing the baby the woman was acting in accordance with the custom of her tribe. It goes against a mother's nature to kill her infant, no matter what is wrong with it. Afterwards, she had been told that under British law she would have to tell the District Commissioner what she had done, so she had walked fifteen miles through the Kikuyu reserve to Nyeri to do what she believed was the right thing. She had concealed nothing. I asked what would happen to her. 'She'll hang,' they told me. So much for British justice.

The policeman who accompanied me to the courthouse told me that I would have to tell the truth as I would have sworn on the Bible to do so. He looked scandalised when I asked, 'But what if you don't believe in God?'

My summons, couched in the archaic language beloved of lawyers the world over, arrived at Seremai the day after the opening of the Erroll murder trial. It read:

To Miss Carberry,
    You are hereby commanded in His Majesty's name to attend the court of [. . .] the 4th day of June 1941 at 10 o'clock in the forenoon or as soon thereafter as the case can be heard as witness in the above case for the defence.
    Dated this 26th day of May 1941.

In the out-turn I was not called.

On 1 July 1941 Broughton was found not guilty. Less than eighteen months later, on 5

December 1942, he killed himself in a Liverpool hotel room. Diana had left him six months earlier.

The loneliness he so feared had caught up with him.

15

Told the Witch-Doctor

A week after my interview with Inspector
Gribble, on 24 February 1941, I left for Malindi
with June and the Rutt.

War had roused the normally sleepy coast into
an unprecedented bustle of military activity. At
the start everyone had assumed the Italians
would attack from the north and rumours
abounded that 200,000 Italians were massed on
the Ethiopian and Somali borders ready to
invade Kenya. The place swarmed with British
and South African troops preparing to repel the
enemy. In June 1940 Italian aircraft had dropped
a couple of bombs on Malindi, damaging some
bee-hives. The only casualties had been the
people who were stung by the bees, for African
bees are rather fierce. In January, just weeks
before we arrived at the coast, British and Allied
troops had entered Italian Somaliland and begun
the pounding which was to end with the capture
of Addis Ababa a few months later and the
occupation of both countries by the end of the
year. In 1942 Mombasa became the base for the
Eastern fleet following the attack on Colombo by
the Japanese. This brought a further influx of
Royal Navy sailors, resplendent in their tropical
whites, on to the island. Mombasa had never
accommodated such a huge white population.

At Malindi the first thing I noticed were th
number of fair-skinned young Englishmen bein
redly roasted by the tropical sun. June and
thought it sexy to be tanned. Our skin was use
to the sun. At first, when we arrived at the coast
I would get little tiny blisters across m
shoulders. They would peel off leaving another
tougher, brown skin underneath. We coul
always tell the Brits. When they undressed to g
swimming their knees would be brown and thei
legs, above and below, chalk white. This wa
caused by their uniform, which was shorts an
long stockings. After a day on the beach thei
legs and feet would be brick red. They used t
spend hours in the water, believing that the se
protected them from the sun. Of course, i
magnifies the rays, as they discovered later.

Malindi's two hotels — Lawfords and th
Sinbad — had been taken over by British troop
The NCOs had access to the Sinbad for thei
meals and drinks, while the officers used th
smarter Lawfords, which was a lovely old hotel

All the European-owned *bandas* had bee
evacuated and placed at the disposal of th
troops, and we found we had a young Britis
officer billeted on us. He was a twenty-three
year-old captain in the Fourth Kings Africa
Rifles called Peter Molloy. While the rest of hi
battalion was still in Mombasa (having com
down from Uganda to the coast at the outbrea
of war to prepare for the anticipated Italia
invasion), Peter had come on ahead with a smal
number of junior officers to build a temporar
camp for the rest of his troop. The job involve

clearing a section of bush and building temporary billets made from *boriti*, the mangrove poles used in construction in traditional coastal architecture, and thatched with *makuti*. June was licking her lips at the prospect of hungry male attention. Once, she followed Peter into the shower, rolling her eyes and bawling out to the Rutt: 'I'm in the shower with him.' June's predatory seductiveness was welcomed by many men, but Peter was romantic and confided to me that June terrified him. To her dismay, Peter preferred me. Not long after that JC came down and Peter moved to another *banda*, which he shared with three other officers, further along the beach.

Ours was young love at its most innocent. Peter came from a good family. He had intended making the army his career and joined the Somerset Light Infantry on leaving Sandhurst. When war was declared he applied to join one of the colonial regiments, which was how he came to be in Kenya. He knew I was not yet sixteen. He also knew that I was unhappy — he could tell from the way she spoke to me what the Rutt was like — and he was too decent to exploit my vulnerability. He was very aware that he might be killed and did not want me to feel too committed. Our feelings for each other were intense, but stopped short at holding hands and kissing. That was when we could be alone together. June and the Rutt did everything they could to prevent it. Whether it was because of the Scottie affair or whether they were jealous because he preferred me, I don't know. Peter

193

would ask June's permission to take me out for a drive, but when he appeared June and the Rutt would climb in with us.

We did manage to lose them one afternoon however. We went for a long walk along the beach to where the Sabaki river, which flowed into the northern end of Malindi Bay, was in flood. In the sea we found a crocodile which had been washed down by the flooded river. It was a bit dopey from having been in salt water for so long. I decided I wanted to use its skin to have a handbag made for June. We had nothing with us to kill it with, so we dragged it along with us by the tail. But its claws dug into the sand. We turned it on to its back but it kept righting itself. It took so long that it was dark by the time we got to the house. Africa was a dangerous place after dark and they'd all been worried that something had happened to 'the brat'. I got into terrible trouble for coming back late. But we managed to kill the crocodile with a handy bit of driftwood and the bag was duly made. I was very disappointed at how little skin there was, but was told only the belly skin is pliable enough to use.

On the way back to Nyeri we stopped in Nairobi for a few days. I took the opportunity of going to see Scottie's mother, who ran a nursing home, and we had tea together. She was very friendly so I don't think she can have realised the trouble I got her son into.

Back at Seremai once more I felt as if I had stepped into a prison cell. The Rutt was more vindictive than ever, spying on me to make sure

194

lidn't go to the Trenches and making trouble for
ne with JC at every opportunity. We were often
eft alone together and one day I decided there
vas only one way out and that was to kill her.
But I didn't want to get found out.

I decided to consult the local *mganga*, or
vitch-doctor, who lived in a round thatched
Kikuyu hut the other side of the Chania river. I
vould ride over to him on Bokkie. This meant
oing down the steep track to the factory and
aking the short-cut road to Nyeri. Horses hated
rossing this bridge as it was made of logs. To
nake it more comfortable for hooves and
ehicles they used to pad it with the fibrous
talks of the sugar cane which were left after the
uice had been extracted. The *mganga* was a
vizened old man with wispy bits of greying hair
ither side of a shiny brown pate. He wore only a
huka, or blanket knotted on one shoulder. Like
ur houseboys he took snuff, which he kept in a
ttle hollowed-out gourd, or calabash, closed
vith a wooden plug and strung on a chain round
is neck. Speaking Swahili, I told him I had
ome to him because I knew African medicine
vas not understood by Europeans. I wanted
ome that would kill a white person but would
e undetectable. Karanga smiled, showing his
appy old teeth, and politely declined to help
ne, explaining that he didn't do bad things.

A few days after our return from Malindi the
Rutt went down with malaria, contracted at the
oast or on the train. June was in Nairobi so, to
ny delight, I realised I had her in my power.
When you have malaria you have to drink as

195

much as you possibly can. I had heard that if you put lemon juice in tin the citric acid caused a poisonous reaction, so I took the hot-water jug we used at tea-time, filled it with lemon juice and waited. After twenty-four hours I decanted the contents into the Rutt's water jug, took it in to her — and waited, hopefully, for her death agony. Alas, she recovered.

Lonely and bored, I next became involved in the most wayward adventure of all. At about this time the farm at Seremai employed a clerk, or *karani*, to take some of the responsibility for supervising and paying the labour off Nellie's hands. He was a Seychellois, with black silky hair and an impenetrable expression in his dark eyes. He was married, with a couple of children, and lived in a stone house with a tin roof halfway down the hill on the way to the factory. I had caught him looking at me and one afternoon while I was in the stable with Bokkie and everyone else was taking a nap, he pounced. There is something very earthy about the smell of hay and straw. Whether they are duchesses with their grooms or peasant wenches with their yokels, girls have been tumbled in the hay since the dawn of time and I did not resist. Now that my bedroom door was no longer locked I could get out at night. I used to hate walking to the stables, terrified that there might be a leopard. But still I went.

We were both playing with fire. I enjoyed defying JC and the Rutt; he probably felt the same. He had a wry sense of humour. He called me his 'angel of death', knowing what his fate would be were his relationship with the *nemsahib kidogo* to be discovered. I liked my *:arani*, but I didn't love him — any more than he loved me.

I kept a diary at this stage of my life. The entry for 20 May 1941 — coded, to keep out prying eyes — reveals that my Sechellois's best-kept plans for safe sex had foundered. There was no access to contraception in those days and coitus interruptus was what most people practised. But the method is famously unreliable. If the Trenches had been around I could have confided in Nellie, but they had gone to the coast, which was five days' drive away. I expressed my fears to my lover and he tried to reassure me, saying that if there was a problem he could get me something to take. Two weeks later, fearing nature might be about to expose our relationship, I tried to find out from Mrs Rowbotham, our housekeeper, what the age of consent was. I had turned sixteen on 7 May. But, remembering the trouble Scottie had found himself in, I was worried about the legal aspect. Social law was clearly not her forte, for my diary note, clearly frustrated, reads: 'Spoke to Mrs Rowbotham about age of consent. 16? 18? ? ? ?'

Now, more than ever, I wanted to get away. It was not just fear of my secret being discovered or the punishments, or that I was constantly afraid. I knew that if I stayed in the Happy Valley environment I would become one of them. I was determined not to.

16

Goodbye Seremai

I knew that if I were patient an opportunity o
getting away from Seremai would present itself
One day June announced that we were off t
Nairobi. She and the Rutt were going to th
races with JC and I was to be parked with Uncl
Gerald, my mother's older brother. I knew
hugging myself in my room, that this would b
my escape.

The only fly in the ointment was a naggin
belief that I was pregnant. I couldn't imagin
raising the possibility of a pregnancy with
religious man like Uncle Gerald. I put th
problem to the back of my mind and immerse
myself in the novelty of life in a norma
household.

Uncle Gerald's home was kind and loving. M
Aunt Caroline was a delightful, gentle perso
and a talented artist, sadly disabled with poli
and confined by that time to a wheelchair. It wa
wonderful to acquire brothers and sister
overnight, having been an only child for so long
Uncle Gerald had five children, three daughter
and two sons. Tony, the eldest daughter, had lef
home and was training to be a doctor, Peter wa
in the army, Patty and Robin, the two younge
daughters, were at university and Robert was sti
at school. None of the Anderson children wa

ver beaten. Since, for the first time in my life, no one had any objection to a girl wanting long hair I began to grow mine. In an excessive reaction to years of repression I went on growing it until it reached four inches below the backs of my knees. Uncle Gerald even sorted out my eyes, taking me to Victor Browse, the leading optician in Nairobi, for a prescription for glasses.

On 22 June I noted in my diary that I went with Uncle Gerald and his family on a trip to Mount Longonot in the Rift valley. The mountain was 2000 feet high and we climbed right to the lip of the crater. Everyone but me had blisters by the time they got there. I was barefoot. I had a few thorns in my feet but I was terribly proud of the fact that I had no blisters. I had a lovely time. It was a family day out of the sort I used to enjoy with the Trenches, before I was banned from visiting them. The Carberrys would never have dreamed of indulging in simple physical pleasures like picnicking or going for a walk in the countryside. For them it always had to be the high life, glass in hand. But children love that sort of thing and I was in my element. Delighted by my new-found happiness I resolved not to let it be taken away from me.

One night when I was alone with Uncle Gerald I pleaded tearfully with him not to send me back to Nyeri, but to allow me to remain in Nairobi permanently. I told him about the dreadful beating and my visit to the police station to display my injuries; of the terror wielded by JC with the Rutt as torturer-in-chief. I begged him to let me stay with him. It was a

responsibility he could have done without. I'm
sure my tears must have stirred painfu
memories. Gerald had known John Carberry fo
over twenty years. Maïa had been his only sistei
He had been aware that she had been unhapp
in her marriage and that she had flown on the
day she was killed only at JC's insistence. Nov
Maïa's child was accusing Carberry of cruelt
beyond belief. Uncle Gerald undertook to speal
to him.

When the two finally talked Carberry'
response was that I could live with my uncle ir
Nairobi, but that if I did so he would cut me of
without a penny. That was a typical reaction. JC
was obsessed with money and assumed everyone
else was, too. People remember him with hi
head constantly buried in the stocks and share
pages of the newspaper. But I have never beer
like that. I didn't hesitate. 'I don't want hi
money,' I told Uncle Gerald truthfully.

One of the good things about leaving Seremai
was that I was able to write to my paterna
grandmother, Mary Carberry, who had stayed ir
touch with the Andersons. I poured out the
whole story of leaving Seremai in a letter to her

In June 1941 I went to the Andersons ir
Nairobi for my holidays and I told them how
hated home, so they kept me. JC and June dic
not seem to mind. JC warned me that if
wanted to live with the Andersons he woulc
cut me out of his will and not give me a thing
that does not worry me a bit because in my
mind happyness [sic] is not bought with

200

money. Well from the 2nd of July 1941 I have been living with Dr Anderson and have been very happy. I have now got 2 brothers and 3 sisters, it is so lovely to feel that I have got a real home and family.

Poor Uncle Gerald. He had a lot less money than the jet-setting John Carberry with his planes and yachts and playboy tastes. And he had five children of his own. He felt I would be coming down in the world. But he was a kind man and a just one. He told me he would not be able to give me much but that I could stay. My heart was so full that I couldn't explain that money without love meant nothing. Instead I said, 'I'll try not to cost you anything.'

July turned into August and I had still not had period. By now I was in a state of panic. I would probably have adopted an ostrich-like attitude to the problem until someone noticed my swelling stomach had not fate taken the matter out of my hands. When JC realised I was not going back to Seremai he agreed to Uncle Gerald's request to send my pony down to Nairobi — he certainly didn't want to be bothered with the expense of a horse. Bokkie had arrived at Nairobi station in a goods van with all his tack, including the rhino whip which the Rutt had used on me. Uncle Gerald lived in a residential area where there was nothing but tarmac underfoot but they rose to the occasion, building Bokkie a shed and letting him graze in the garden. On 30 August I was riding into town when the pony shied at something, slipped on the tarmac and came down on top of me. The force of the fall produced what I had been praying for.

By the time Uncle Gerald came home I had lost the baby and was bleeding profusely.

Uncle Gerald realised immediately that he was witnessing a miscarriage. He tried very hard to find out who was responsible but all I would say was that the father was one of June's South African boyfriends and that I didn't know his name. Gerald was concerned about me, of that have no doubt. He wasn't fierce or censorious but he was a religious man and was also clearly anxious about his own good name and the social consequences for him should any scandal get out. To my great relief I never became pregnant again. I may not have got on with John Carberry but we did share a distaste for breeding.

It says a lot for Uncle Gerald that in spite of the shock my pregnancy must have given him he decided to adopt me.

JC was a predictably bad loser. Despite having no feelings for me he was furious with his brother-in-law for taking me in, in what must have seemed to him a very public gesture of reproof. Having always loathed religion in all its forms, Carberry must have found it particularly humiliating to have been morally wrong-footed by someone as devoutly Christian as Uncle Gerald. Hurt pride doubtless lay behind the outraged letter with which he responded to my uncle's proposal, some months later, to adopt me. The tail contains a sting of wit not normally associated with John Carberry.

Seremai,
Nyeri,
Nov 25th 1941

Dear Gerald,

In signing the agreement drawn up by Mr Kaplan re. yourself and Juanita, I should like the said agreement to be taken in conjunction with the following letter.

The whole question of whether Juanita should leave her legal parent and guardian, in other words myself, was raised by you, no doubt acting in good faith to the best of your belief, but from our point of view I feel that this change has been due almost entirely to the misrepresentation of facts by Juanita herself and the various lies she has spread around about her life here with us.

Although legally I believe you will agree with me from what you have been told by your legal advisor, that were you to endeavour to force us to give Juanita up to yourself or some branch of the Anderson family, you would have a very poor chance of succeeding. You promised to produce affidavits and witnesses to support your allegations but these have never materialised, and, as far as we are concerned, they do not exist. But we on our part feel very bitter about all the malicious chatter that Juanita has spread around very ably supported by our nearest neighbour [Maxwell Trench], and we feel that if she chooses to make a rough bed for herself for the future, it is not our business to stop her

203

lying on it. Therefore, rather than expose al
concerned to a mud-slinging lawsuit, w
propose to relinquish custody of Juanita t
yourself, and we intend to send a copy of thi
correspondence to her remaining guardian i
the USA.

I regret that you seem quite willing to sel
your niece's birthright for a mess of pottag
served up on an 'Oxford platter' complete witl
'Christian salad' and 'Buchmanite dressing'.
    Sincerely,
    John Carberry

These jibes in the final paragraph are a sneerin
reference by John Carberry, an avowed atheist, t
my uncle's religious beliefs, for Uncle Geral
was a member of the Oxford Group, a Christia
evangelistic movement set up in the Twenties b
the American preacher Frank N. Buchman.

I saw this letter for the first time fifty-seve
years after it was written, while working on thi
book. What I noticed is that Carberry canno
bring himself to use the word 'father', despit
playing to the full the part of the injured parent

If Carberry's display of self-righteous bluste
was designed to intimidate Uncle Gerald i
failed. On 31 December 1941, just over a montl
after his original letter, John Evans Carberry
'Settler of Nyeri', signed an agreement accordin
to which Gerald Anderson undertook to adopt
'female child known as Juanita Maïa Sistani [sic
upon certain terms and conditions'. I wa
amused to note that, ever the attentive parent
and notwithstanding the importance he attache

204

o orthographic niceties in his own life (being Mr ohn Carberry with two 'r's and not Lord Carberry with one), JC had overlooked the two mistakes in my names — my middle name was 'irginia not Maïa and I was Sistare not Sistani. The conditions of my adoption included Uncle Gerald paying for everything involving my care until I reached twenty-one. He was solemnly enjoined to 'bring up the infant in a manner ordinarily considered suitable for the child of a parent occupying the social position of the adopter and will provide the infant with all things necessary or proper for her in that position and endeavour to promote her welfare and advancement in the world'. In the light of the heedless way my upbringing had been handled at Nyeri this was irony indeed. Carberry's signature was witnessed by the Rutt, my hated governess, who signed herself 'Isabel Rutt. Spinster'.

Most of the changes I found at Uncle Gerald's were welcome. At Seremai there was an atmosphere of decadence and idleness, no one ever had a job to go to, alcohol under-pinned all social relationships and created a culture whose hallmarks were loud rowing and swearing, and uninhibited sexual horseplay, which I found deeply distasteful. Uncle Gerald was a hard-working surgeon and a member of a deeply religious sect, which was strictly teetotal. His family kept normal hours and I cannot remember anyone ever raising his or her voice, let alone using swear-words.

One change I didn't care for, however, was the

Andersons' repressive attitude towards se
which, like their aversion to alcohol, was
spin-off of their religious beliefs. I had grown u
on a farm and had observed nature at work fror
a very young age. Moreover, at Seremai, Jun
and the Rutt had been so busy feeding their ow:
sexual appetites they'd had little inclination t
mount guard over the brat's virtue and I'
become used to plenty of freedom. At Uncl
Gerald's house, Victorian-style prudishness ha·
created a climate of ignorance which shocke·
me. My cousin Robin, who was the same age a
me, was going out with a boy called Ronni
Harris.

One night she came up to bed in a state c
some anxiety. 'Do you think I'm going to have
baby?'

'Why? What have you been doing?'

'I kissed Ronnie good night.'

'But then what happened?'

Only when she assured me that a kiss was th
climax of Ronnie's ardour did I realise that thi
sixteen-year-old doctor's daughter was totall
ignorant of the facts of life.

Uncle Gerald clearly felt I would benefit fror
exposure to religion. JC had alluded, through th
sarcastic coda he added to the end of th
adoption certificate, to Gerald Anderson'
involvement with the Oxford Group's rathe
evangelical interpretation of Christianity. Th
group were committed to raising the mor:
tone of all aspects of twentieth-century societ
from employer–worker relations to internation:
affairs, and called themselves Moral Rearmamen

206

n an allusion to the physical rearmament that preoccupied the industrialised world between the wars. I was invited to join some of the Moral Rearmament meetings, which were held in the sitting-room of Uncle Gerard's house. Fellow group members would take it in turns to confess their misdemeanours publicly. The meetings were renowned for breaking up a lot of marriages as people used to come out with admissions of adultery in this open confessional. The sessions I attended were a lot less juicy. The sins' ranged from the awesomely pedestrian to the startlingly personal. One man announced: 'I was a bit short with my wife yesterday. It was unkind of me. I didn't know she had her period.' On another occasion Uncle Gerald and Aunt Caroline were pondering which school to send their youngest child, Robert, to. Deciding to invoke the power of prayer, they gave each of us a piece of paper and told us to write on it the name of the school we thought Robert ought to attend. As far as I was concerned the meetings reached the zenith of absurdity when we were joined by an elderly woman called Audrey. Calling for a time of quiet before opening the meeting, Uncle Gerald addressed the Almighty: 'And thank you, Lord, for letting Audrey come to tea.' I found it not merely odd, but tasteless, that a group of adults could bury their heads in this kind of triviality when there was a world war raging all around us.

While I endeavoured to adjust to my somewhat conventional new life, Uncle Gerald was discovering the fathomless depths of my ignorance — and wondering how best to counter it. It was my inability to make any sense of columns of figures which first alerted him. He located a private maths teacher and sent me for lessons with her. She lived near Nairobi Railway Club, which was one of the many social clubs in the city.

I had to ride there and back. One day the teacher gave me a note addressed to Uncle Gerald. Being both wayward and incurably curious I opened it. It read:

Dear Gerald,

I cannot possibly take your money. There is no way I can teach Maths to this child.

Knowing the unconventional upbringing I had endured, Uncle Gerald had wanted to keep me at home and curb my wild ways by surrounding me with the stability of a caring family life. Reading this, he must have realised it was not going to be possible. It was decided that from the start of 1942 I should attend the rather select, and doubtless very expensive, Wykeham Girls School in Pietermaritzburg, in Natal.

Something had to be done about my ignorance in the meantime, though. At the end of October I was packed off to a small private school, which was run from a cattle ranch out in the plains fifty miles from Nairobi on the Mombasa side. The ranch was at Konza and was called Kalanzoni. The school, which was attended by only a handful of girls, was run by a woman called Tilly Button whose husband

Ernest managed the ranch.

The ranch house was built of cedar wood to protect it from being eaten by termites but that didn't prevent it becoming infested with ticks which came off the dogs. Lessons never made much impression on me. What I loved was the wonderful isolation. We were miles from any kind of civilisation. It was real frontier living and I adored it. I was allowed to have Bokkie, who came out on the train from Nairobi and stepped out of his goods wagon at Konza station as calmly as if he'd been travelling on trains all his life. I never tired of the thrill of seeing lions when we were out on horseback.

The neighbouring ranch was owned by Blaney Percival, one of Africa's best-known white hunters. Percival had a daughter called Gugie who became a great friend and a son called Buster. Gugie was in the army and it was because of her that I decided I would join the FANYs (First Aid Nursing Yeomanry) as soon as was old enough. I used to ride over to their ranch, which was called Mumandu, and go buck hunting with Buster for the pot and to feed the dogs. Sadly, Buster was killed when the troopship *Kalid Ismael* that was taking him from Mombasa to Ceylon was torpedoed.

Another activity we enjoyed was making riems. These are strips of cowhide used as yokes for the ox wagons which do all the work in Africa. To make the cowhide — or rawhide, as it was called — supple you twisted it round and round, and then attached a heavy weight to the end. We used whatever came to hand, often a

wheel hub. The idea was to keep it twisting firs
one way and then the other till it became sof
and pliable.

I left the Button ranch at Christmas an
stayed with the Andersons till the end of Januar
1942. I was dreading going off to school agai
and I was indeed very homesick for the first fev
weeks. With the prospect of a year away I ha
had to sell my beloved Bokkie, for in built-u
Nairobi there were no horsy neighbours t
exercise him for me. I replaced him with
youngster who would not be ready for breakin
until I got back, but he came to a sad end.
poured out my feelings to Granny Carberry.

I hated leaving, but it was for my own goo·
and only for one year. The day I left home
sold my pony to some terribly nice people an·
bought a new 18 months old Arab pony whic·
I wanted to leave at home to get used to th
surroundings and traffic so that I could brea
him in and train him when I got back; he wa
a really beautiful animal and terribly intelli
gent and good-natured. About a month ago
terribly bad horse disease broke out and ton
of horses have died and my pony died to [sic]
it nearly broke my heart, because he was s·
adorable, and it will be ages before I will b
able to save up enough to buy a good nev
pony like him, and as we are now so short o
petrol I was hoping to save up for a trap an·
harness, although I don't know where I coul·
get a trap from.

Now that I was free of the Carberry jurisdiction I wrote regularly to my grandmother and, to my great delight, was also in touch again with the Trenches. As Nellie Trench was at Jadini it was decided I should spend some ten days with her before embarking on the Imperial Airways flying boat in which I was to travel south to Durban from Mombasa on 5 February. It was lovely being with the motherly Nellie once more, knowing that never again could the Rutt spoil things. She was very emotional on seeing me. If I had suffered through JC's treatment of me, so had Nellie and Maxwell. Poor Nellie blamed herself for not having adopted me after my mother's death. She and Maxwell had thought that JC's money would give me a better life and had hoped that June would be a mother to me. Nellie might have had another more personal reason for wanting to adopt me but I didn't know this at the time.

★   ★   ★

To have travelled by flying boat seems a wonderfully glamorous experience from another age. The first flying boat service flew out of Southampton bound for Durban in 1937. It was a far more expensive way of reaching Durban than steamer, but Uncle Gerald may have felt obliged to make this rather lavish gesture. By 1942 travelling down the East African coast by sea was becoming increasingly dangerous as the Japanese had torpedoed a number of ships. The Short Empire flying boats, which were built in

211

Ireland, aimed to be the airborne equivalent o
the luxury ocean liner. Their design allowed the
traveller more space than was possible in a
conventional aircraft. We sat in seats which faced
each other, with a table in between. The colou
scheme in the one I travelled on was a pleasing
beige and blue. The food, which was freshly
cooked on board, was delicious, and the ladies
room was like something out of a luxury hotel
with a self-contained lavatory, a wash-basin and
a mirrored dressing-table on which were placed a
variety of pots and bottles containing cotton
wool, powder, face-cream and eau-de-toilette.

Seaplanes ceased flying in 1950. Their lack o
versatility was already starting to make them
look old-fashioned. Not only did they have to
keep landing to refuel, but they could land only
where there was water. During the journey
which was almost two thousand miles, we
stopped at Dar es Salaam and Lindi in what was
then Tanganyika, and Beira and Lourenço-
Marques in Portuguese Mozambique, before
landing in Durban. We broke the journey at
Lourenço-Marques and stayed in a hote
overnight.

Pietermaritzburg was known as sleepy hollow
because it was seen as a provincial backwater
lacking the sophisticated fleshpots of Durban or
Johannesburg. At the ultra-conventional Wykeham School (motto: manners maketh man), I
acquired a new identity and a new religion.
Juanita Carberry was now reborn as Juanita
Anderson. This was designed to protect my
reputation, as I embarked at my new school,

rom association with a scandal involving John Carberry.

After I had left Nyeri, Carberry had fallen foul of the authorities and landed up in prison. All mail was being censored because of the war and a cable from John Carberry to the United States urging the sale of lucrative US aircraft shares had been intercepted. Defence share values always boom in wartime and Carberry had intended to make a killing. To add insult to injury he was dealing with an agent based in Lourenço-Marques whom he knew to be working for the Germans. This was a flagrant breach of Defence Finance Regulations. All British citizens were required to declare dollar assets to the authorities who needed the American currency to fund the war effort. Such unpatriotic profiteering was viewed in a dim light in wartime and JC was sentenced to two years' hard labour. He managed to get the sentence halved on appeal and ended up serving one year in Fort Jesus, the old fortress in Mombasa. In fact, as there weren't many white men in prison, JC stayed in the prison governor's house. There he led the life of a country gentleman rather than a convict, getting meals and champagne sent in from the Mombasa Club, which was a stone's throw from Fort Jesus, and spending the days playing bridge, a game he was passionate about, with three other prisoners. He was considerably put out when one of his fellow inmates was hanged as it meant he no longer had a four for bridge.

June Carberry, who was no more patriotic

than JC, thought the whole thing a huge joke. She sent all her friends telegrams proclaiming: 'Pop's in the cooler.'

I said I discovered a new religion at Wykeham. JC had instructed every school I attended that I was to be exempt from all scripture lessons and I had been grateful to him for this. Uncle Gerald was a religious man, however, so there were no more exemptions. Every Sunday all the Wykeham girls, quaintly dressed in our navy gymslips, black stockings and straw boaters, trooped off to church in a long crocodile. I discovered that two girls who came from the Seychelles were Catholic. They were allowed to walk by themselves to the Catholic church nearby and got special food on Fridays. I became a Catholic which, in fact, was what I had been baptised. We discovered that there were young lads from the Polish army stationed nearby who were also Catholic and we used to set off for church early so we could meet them and go for a cuddle and a cigarette. Then they used to walk part of the way back to school with us.

Swimming was still the only activity I excelled at. I described my triumphs to Mary Carberry: 'During the Summer we had swimming, I entered for all the public matches, and won several prizes, and also I was put into the school team almost as soon as I got here which was very nice as I often swam for the school and also once for Natal.'

The beating regime of June and JC had purported to teach me the lesson that to lie is a mistake. At Wykeham I learned that it can be a mistake to tell the truth. At the Christmas carol service it was the custom to modify the words 'While Shepherds Watched their Flocks by Night', in the manner of children since the carol was first written to 'While Shepherds Washed their Socks by Night'. This caused a terrible furore. All girls singing the frivolous words were told to raise their hands. I instantly obeyed — only to realise to my surprise that mine was the only hand up. I was punished by being stopped from riding.

The distance from Pietermaritzburg to Nairobi was too far to hop home for all the holidays. Two of my new 'sisters' were in the south, Patty at Cape Town University and Robin at Rhodes University in Salisbury. It was Uncle Gerald's idea that we should link up and spend the Easter holidays in an improving environment. The Swedish medical missionaries with whom we stayed lived at Mapumulo in Zululand. While I was there I discovered some books which contained gruesome coloured illustrations of the ravages venereal disease inflicted on the human body. I found them riveting but when I was caught reading them the missionaries were mortified. The missionaries weren't horsy people but there were police horses in the neighbourhood, great big animals, quite different from the ponies I rode in Kenya, and I rode them.

The next holidays I spent with Zia Simmonds, the head girl of Wykeham. Her parents had a farm on the Mooi river in Natal. They had horses so we spent our days riding and helping with work on the farm. They also had a tame crested crane called Awang after the shrill peacock-like call he made. If you bent down he would hop up on your back.

At Christmas I was allowed to return to Nairobi. Instead of taking the seaplane, I travelled by Rhodesia Airways. In those days we had to stop to refuel at Salisbury (Southern Rhodesia), Lusaka, Mpika (Northern Rhodesia), and Mbeya and Dodoma (Tanganyika). We spent the night at Mbeya, where my vanity landed me in trouble. I had got chatting to a boy the same age as me on the plane. He knew there was a pool at Mbeya and suggested we go for a swim. The first thing I did whenever I was trying to look attractive was 'lose' my glasses. We arrived at the pool and went into our separate changing rooms. I planned to wear a bikini but when I unpacked I found I'd only got the bottom with me. I had obviously left the top in the hotel. I dressed and went out to look for my date, but without glasses I couldn't recognise him. He finally found me and was annoyed that I was still fully dressed when I had been so eager for a swim. I felt too foolish to explain the real cause of the confusion.

In May 1942 I turned seventeen. At last the end of my years of school were in sight. I had promised Uncle Gerald that I would not be a financial burden to him and looked forward to joining the army and earning my own living. Although hardly feeling grown-up, I was keen to see the back of my childhood, to be able to be my own woman, to be free of both Happy Valley

216

dissolution and Moral Rearmament restrictions. On 2 February 1943 I enlisted in the Women's Territorial Service. The FANY mess, which was to be my home for the duration of the war, was in the requisitioned Loreto Convent on the outskirts of Nairobi, near the Kabete Road. (The uniform of khaki skirts — which had to be fourteen inches off the ground — khaki stockings, khaki battle bloomers — which in my case reached from my knees to my underarms — and clodhopper shoes did not please some of the glamour pusses.) In joining the FANYs I closed the chapter on my strange precocious childhood. At Seremai, at Malindi, at Muthaiga Club, the last remnants of Happy Valley partied on, little knowing that their story, too, had reached its final pages. The wind of change would soon be blowing, a cold, unforgiving gale that would sweep them — *bwanas, memsahibs,* pink gins and all — out of Africa and into the pages of history.

The next few years would find me joining a circus, driving a taxi and enlisting in the Merchant Navy at a time when only two British cargo ships out of the entire fleet took women. But that's another story . . .

Epilogue: It's a Wise Child Who Knows Its Own Father

Was John Carberry's lack of affection for me simply due to his warped personality — or was there a reason for it?

I met him once when I was grown-up. What he said then raised a question which has remained unanswered. I was sitting in the Avenue Hotel in Nairobi when Carberry walked in. I had been swimming competitively for the army.

In the American drawl he affected, he commented on my success, which had been reported in the press: 'But I didn't see you listed in the diving competitions.'

'No. I don't dive.'

'Is that my fault?'

'I don't know.'

'Do you think I was cruel to you as a child?'

'Cruelty is a very difficult word to define. Let's say you never acted as a fond parent.'

'That's because I wasn't your father.'

If it was his excuse for mistreating me I thought it a poor one. 'Well, you were in a position to act as my father and you never did.'

I told the Andersons of JC's claim. Gerald was furious. He saw it as a slur on his dead sister's name and wanted to take Carberry to court.

Some years later I was in a private sitting-room at Claridge's hotel, making somewhat

218

stilted conversation with my godmother. Over tea and cucumber sandwiches Aunt Sistare suddenly asked, 'What is Maxwell Trench like?'

'Why do you ask?'

'Well, you know he was your father?'

I was very taken aback. I suspected Aunt Sistare had seen JC recently. Had she criticised him for ill-treating me and was this his lame defence? Or was I really the product of an illicit romance between Maxwell and Maïa? That would explain certain things, such as temperamental similarities, JC's coldness and my sense of belonging at the Trenches'. When I next saw Nellie Trench I tackled her about it. She neither confirmed nor denied Carberry's claim. 'You can think what you like,' she said, but she repeated how much she and Maxwell had wanted to adopt me when Maïa was killed. And she told me about Maxwell's other daughter in Jamaica, the product of a liaison he had had with a house servant, whom he acknowledged and maintained.

While I was at sea I was taken ill and put off in Trinidad. Nellie Trench cabled me to seek out Olive Dwyer, the head of nursing at the hospital in Port of Spain. Olive was Maxwell's daughter. I have known Olive for many years. She has become a friend. I have also become friendly with Jo Claridge, who is John Carberry's daughter by his first marriage to José Metcalfe.

One of them is my sister — but which? While writing this book I contacted a DNA laboratory to ask whether, if all three women agreed to give samples, we might find out who did father me. I was advised that, since no DNA from either putative father was available, it was unlikely we would get a conclusive answer. And so the grave has kept my mother's secret. To me it doesn't matter a jot. I'm neither Carberry's child nor Trench's child. I'm me. Olive and Jo are relieved, because, in a response that I find touching, this way they feel they can both continue to claim me.

★　★　★

John Carberry died in 1970 in South Africa, the favoured refuge for many Kenya whites in flight from the bloody Mau Mau uprising of the Fifties. In a bizarre echo of my mother's death, I didn't learn of JC's until two years later, when a woman I knew slightly offered me her condolences. The circumstances of his demise have a Gothic aspect which, in view of his lifelong respect for money, might have amused him. He died on the twenty-first of the month. As the endowment was payable on a quarter day, which was the twenty-fifth, June put his body in the deep freeze to preserve it (in that climate a vital precaution) to enable a sympathetic doctor to issue the death certificate on the 'right' day.

June Carberry died five years later. Still drinking and smoking, she had grown into the proverbial rich, dotty old lady. Her love of dogs had become an obsession. She would drive out into Johannesburg looking for strays, followed by a second car, driven by her African chauffeur, into which the waifs would be placed when located. If the dogs were ill they would be tenderly wrapped in June's mink coat. When she died I was sent a copy of her will. What was left of John Carberry's fortune was divided between June's hairdresser, her chauffeur, a dogs' home and the South African Wildlife Society.

Isabel Rutt left John Carberry's employment soon after I decamped to the Andersons in June 1941 and went to teach at Pembroke House, a boys' school in Gilgil, where she is remembered by former pupils as stern and humourless. She retired to England.

It was my destiny to grow up among a small group of people whose reputation for behaving badly has earned them a place in the history of colonialism. The Happy Valley set was a unique phenomenon. Shallow, spoiled and self-centred, they were by nature metropolitan consumers who, set down in the Garden of Eden, found it dull. Beneath the froth of the dancing, the drinking, the overt liaisons, there lurked an element of the frantic. Many became addicts, either of drink or drugs. The cheap cost of living bestowed the kind of comforts only enjoyed by the super-rich at home; there was no nine-to-five routine to regularise their life and blunt their energy; as for setting an example, who cared, with only the natives watching? The images of June Carberry and her friends downing yet more drinks, heedless of the servants trying anxiously to save the roast which is already hours late, of Lady Idina parading naked in front of her servant, tell the story.

The people who built the colony were very different. They were doughty, decent men and women who earned their sundowners by the sweat of their brow and left farms, hospitals, hotels, businesses, newspaper empires behind a a testament to their industry.

It had begun with such confidence. Theodore Roosevelt had proclaimed that 'there is, here in Africa under the Equator a real white man' country'. Joseph Chamberlain said: 'This coun try . . . will one day be one of the greatest and best of the British Empire.'

In the out-turn it had lasted barely half a century. By the Sixties the workers and the worthless alike had been swept aside by the irresistible tide of history.

I went back to Seremai some years ago. It was still a coffee farm, but the house was neglected and shabby. The parquet floor in the drawing room had not seen polish for many a year; the room where my governess the Rutt had played the grand piano and June Carberry had smooched with a succession of boyfriends was piled high with sacks of coffee. Goats grazed on what had been the lawn and the flower beds had long since been reclaimed by weeds. It was a though John Carberry — his planes, his yacht his Riviera holidays — and a small girl who played happily with the African *totos* had never been.

★   ★   ★

When I was recalling often painful details of my long-ago childhood for this book, Diana Francis-Jones, the grand-daughter of Maxwell

Trench, who is a dear friend, sent me the following poem. Its wry tone appeals to me.

'This Be The Verse' by Philip Larkin, from *Collected Poems*

They fuck you up, your mum and dad.
They may not mean to, but they do.
They fill you with the faults they had
And add some extra, just for you.

But they were fucked up in their turn
By fools in old-style hats and coats,
Who half the time were soppy-stern
And half at one another's throats.

Man hands on misery to man.
It deepens like a coastal shelf.
Get out as early as you can,
And don't have any kids yourself.

(. . . *and I didn't.*)

We do hope that you have enjoyed reading
this large print book.

Did you know that all of our titles
are available for purchase?

We publish a wide range of high quality
large print books including:
Romances, Mysteries, Classics
General Fiction
Non Fiction and Westerns

Special interest titles available in
large print are:
The Little Oxford Dictionary
Music Book
Song Book
Hymn Book
Service Book

Also available from us courtesy of Oxford
University Press:
Young Readers' Dictionary
(large print edition)
Young Readers' Thesaurus
(large print edition)

For further information or a free
brochure, please contact us at:
Ulverscroft Large Print Books Ltd.,
The Green, Bradgate Road, Anstey,
Leicester, LE7 7FU, England.
Tel: (00 44) 0116 236 4325
Fax: (00 44) 0116 234 0205

Other titles in the
Charnwood Library Series:

LOVE ME OR LEAVE ME

Josephine Cox

Beautiful Eva Bereton has only three friends
in the world: Patsy, who she looks upon as a
sister; Bill, her adopted cousin, and her
mother, to whom she is devoted. With Eva's
father increasingly angry about life as a
cripple, she and her mother support each
other, keeping their spirits high despite the
abuse. So when a tragic accident robs Eva of
both parents, Patsy, a loveable Irish rogue, is
the only one left to support her. Tragedy
strikes yet again when Eva's uncle comes to
reclaim the farm that Eva had always believed
belonged to her parents. Together with Patsy,
Eva has no choice but to start a new life far
away . . .

COLDITZ: THE GERMAN STORY

Reinhold Eggers

This is the story of the famous German prison camp Colditz — as the German guards saw it. It was a place where every man felt that in spite of the personal tragedy of imprisonment, it was his duty to overcome. The book vividly describes the constant battle of wits between guards and prisoners, the tunnelling, bribery, impersonations, forgery and trickery of all kinds by which brave men sought to return to the war.

FALSE PRETENCES

Margaret Yorke

When her goddaughter is arrested during an anti-roads protest, Isabel Vernon is startled to discover that the fair-haired child of her memory has become a shaven-headed environmentalist and that Isabel herself is now regarded as Emily Frost's next of kin. Emily, released on bail to the Vernons, takes up a job as home help to a local family and forms an instant attachment to Rowena, the four-year-old girl in her charge. Emily's presence in the Vernons' house proves troubling, and is deepening the profound tensions within Isabel's marriage when the arrival of someone else threatens the safety of both Emily and the child, Rowena.

GRAND AFFAIR

Charlotte Bingham

Unaware of the misery that surrounded her birth, for the first four years of her life all Ottilie Cartaret knows is love. And when her mother, Ma O'Flaherty, moves her family to St Elcombe in Cornwall, their fortunes seem set fair. However, Ma tragically dies and Ottilie is adopted by the Cartarets, who run the Grand Hotel. The little girl grows up pampered and spoilt, not only by her adoptive parents but by all the visitors — with the exception of their mysterious annual guest, nicknamed 'Blue Lady'. But as times change and the regular vistors die off, only Ottilie can save the now-decaying hotel.

THE DEATH ZONE

Matt Dickinson

Ten expeditions were high on Everest, preparing for their summit push. They set out in perfect conditions on 10 May 1996. But twenty-four hours later, eight climbers were dead and a further three were to die, victims of one of the most devastating storms ever to hit the mountain. On the North Face, a British expedition found itself in the thick of the drama. Against all the odds, film-maker Matt Dickinson and professional climber Alan Hinkes managed to battle through hurricane-force winds to reach the summit. This is Matt Dickinson's extraordinary story of human triumph, folly and disaster.

STILL WATER

John Harvey

The naked body of a young woman is found floating in an inner-city canal. Not the first, nor the last. When another woman disappears, following a seminar on women and violence, everyone fears for her safety — especially those who know about her husband's controlling character. Is this a one-off domestic crime or part of a wider series of murders? What else has been simmering beneath this couple's apparently normal middle-class life? As Resnick explores deeper, he finds disturbing parallels between the couple he's investigating and his own evolving relationship with Hannah Campbell.